BEYOND THE LION'S DEN

BEYOND THE LION'S DEN

BEYOND THE LION'S DEN

KEN SHAMROCK WITH ERICH KRAUSS

TUTTLE PUBLISHING
Tokyo • Rutland, Vermont • Singapore

Dedication

To my wife Tonya,
and my father Bob

First published in 2005 by Tuttle Publishing, an imprint of
Periplus Editions (HK) Ltd., with editorial offices at
364 Innovation Drive, North Clarendon, VT 05759.

Library of Congress Control Number: 2005923059
ISBN: 0-8048-3659-0

Please note that the publisher and author(s) of this instructional
book are NOT RESPONSIBLE in any manner whatsoever for any
injury that may result from practicing the techniques and/or following the instructions given within. Martial arts training can be
dangerous—both to you and to others—if not practiced safely. If
you're in doubt as to how to proceed or whether your practice is
safe, consult with a trained martial arts teacher before beginning.
Since the physical activities described herein may be too strenuous
in nature for some readers, it is also essential that a physician be
consulted prior to training.

DISTRIBUTED BY

North America, Latin America & Europe
Tuttle Publishing
364 Innovation Drive
North Clarendon, VT 05759-9436
Tel: (802) 773-8930
Fax: (802) 773-6993
info@tuttlepublishing.com
www.tuttlepublishing.com

Japan
Tuttle Publishing
Yaekari Building, 3rd Floor
5-4-12 Ōsaki
Shinagawa-ku
Tokyo 141 0032
Tel: (03) 5437-0171
Fax: (03) 5437-0755
tuttle-sales@gol.com

Asia Pacific
Berkeley Books Pte. Ltd.
130 Joo Seng Road
#06-01/03 Olivine Building
Singapore 368357
Tel: (65) 6280-1330
Fax: (65) 6280-6290
inquiries@periplus.com.sg
www.periplus.com

First edition
08 07 06 05   10 9 8 7 6 5 4 3 2 1

Printed in Singapore

Contents

PART ONE
From Rage to Redemption

1

The Road to the Ring

I CLIMB INTO A STEEL CAGE AND FIGHT; that's what I do for a living. Some people have a hard time with that. They don't understand how I can slam an opponent to the ground, climb on top of him, and then beat him unconscious with punches, knees, and elbows. They don't understand how I can give that same opponent a respectful hug or handshake when he wakes up. The explanation really isn't that complicated. First of all, I'm a born athlete and competitor. I thrive off the thrill of battle, and when it comes to hand-to-hand combat, you won't find any tougher battles than you do in the rings and cages of mixed martial arts competition. Second, the sport allows me to channel my rage into something positive, and in my eyes, that is nothing short of a miracle.

I didn't begin this life on a very positive note. As one of the only white kids growing up in an all-black neighborhood of Savannah, Georgia, during the late 1960s, I found myself brawling in the schoolyard, brawling in the park, brawling all the neighborhood kids who wanted to drop kick me in the head and turn my pockets inside out. Just as fighting became a way of life, my family moved away from the ghetto and settled in Napa, a city in California's wine country where young boys didn't need to fight for their survival. I tried to be normal,

but a switch had been flipped in my head and I couldn't turn it off. I got in trouble at school and with the cops, so I ran away and lived in an abandoned car parked behind a convenience store. Then one night an older runaway tried to stab me in the face with a locked blade. While I was in the hospital getting stitched up, a couple of cops dropped by to haul me kicking and screaming down to juvenile hall. I was ten years old at that point. I spent six months locked up with seventeen-year-old men who'd done hard time in California Youth Authority. I fought, always fought, but most nights it was hard to sleep because of the lumps on my face and the blood draining down the back of my throat. When I got out, it was off to a string of group homes, each one worse than the last. So I spent some time on the street, and then I spent some more time in juvenile hall. I learned how my body could be used to hurt people to survive.

Eventually I landed in my adopted father's group home, Bob Shamrock's Group Home for Boys, and I found a home and people who cared about me. I built a life for myself, but all that rage was still bottled up, still searching for a way to escape. It haunted me for ten solid years, and it wasn't until I stepped into a ring and engaged in battle—a battle that had no rules—that I finally found a release for all my anger and rage. I no longer had to get into scraps out in the street; I no longer wanted to.

I took the ball and ran, never looked back. It was the best decision I have ever made. Competing in mixed martial arts (MMA) competition has allowed me to walk through life proud of who I am and what I have accomplished. Without it, I don't know what I would have done. But finding the path I was meant to travel didn't happen overnight. Between the time that I left my adopted father's group home and the time I had my first professional fight at twenty-seven, there were ten years of soul searching, ten years of jumping from one job to the next in hopes of finding my niche.

That long and winding road began with bouncing in bars at eighteen years of age. Although I was well below the legal age limit to work in the bar, it's amazing what a reputation can do for you. I was already known as "One Punch Shamrock" by that point. It's not that I went out looking for fights, but in the sunny small town of Susanville, California, fights came looking for you. This was especially true if you were one of the city slickers being raised in Bob Shamrock's group home. A lot of our guys came from gangs in the city. They wore flannel shirts with only the top button fastened and strutted from place to place. Needless to say, the young cowboys in town didn't like us invading their turf. They despised everything about us, and I guess I can't really blame them. After all, we stole all their women.

So there were some fights between the local rednecks and us hoodlums. Actually, it would better be described as a war, and I happened to win a majority of the battles in that war. And when I wasn't fighting

cowboys, I was fighting anyone else who stepped up to me. I beat up this one kid who happened to be dating an ex-girlfriend of mine. He was pissed off about something or other, and he skipped a beer bottle across the hood of my father's car, a mint '57 Eldorado. If you knew my father, you'd know how much he loves his cars. I happened to be the caretaker of that car for the day, so my anger went through the roof. I hit the kid so hard I literally knocked him out of his shoes. Another time, a couple buddies and I were sitting in a parking lot when a group of college baseball players came up and accused us of throwing something at their car. We hadn't thrown anything at their car, so when they pressed the issue, I solved the matter with my fists. Even when I broke my neck on the high school wrestling mats and had a god-awful halo bolted to my head, I was still scrapping at the drop of a dime. As I already mentioned, something had snapped in my mind at a very young age and I couldn't seem to turn it off.

My name started getting around. By the time I graduated from high school, people had heard about me two hours in every direction. It's probably not something I should have been proud of, but I was. I wasn't the best in school, and I didn't know where I was headed or how long it would take to get there. My fists were something to count on, something that made me stand out. And besides, my reputation as a brawler got me a job bouncing in a bar three years before the law allowed.

At first sweeping the floor with barroom drunks was only a way to pay the bills. I was going to be a professional football player, end of story. I had done well on the high school field, and I wanted to jump right to the pros. When I realized that achieving such a goal was highly unlikely, I enrolled at Shasta Community College near my home to play ball, even though school was the last place I wanted to be. I played inside linebacker for two years, but because I had neglected to sit through even a few of my classes, I didn't earn enough credit to go on to a university. Just as I was beginning to wonder if I might never fulfill my dream of playing with the pros, I got drafted by the Sacramento Bulldogs. It was a semipro team, but it seemed to me like I was halfway there.

It didn't take long for me to realize the semipro ball was not even close to being in the same league as professional football. It was basically just a bunch of weekend warriors who got together to practice a couple of times a week, and the paychecks were so minimal they hardly put food on the table. So it was back to the bars, only now I was working in some of the big clubs over in Reno, which was just an hour or so drive from my home. I wasn't all that happy about where I was or what I was doing. I was searching for something exciting, something to get my blood pumping, and then I heard about this Toughman competition they were having over in Redding, California. I was still bouncing in a couple of clubs in Redding, and since it wouldn't be that far of a drive, I thought I would enter the tournament and see what it was all about.

I had no official fight training at that point, just what I had learned on the street. I didn't have a flawless right cross or a string of savage combinations tucked away in my arsenal. But I did have several advantages over my opponents. First, I was strong. I had always been strong, and having fought for so long in the street, I knew how to use that strength to my advantage. Second, I had no fear. You would think that climbing into a ring in front of hundreds of people and putting your pride on the line would make a twenty-year-old kid nervous, but it didn't. I felt just as comfortable in the ring as I did walking down the street. No sweaty palms, no cotton mouth. Nothing but a chest full of rage.

Although my first two competitors outweighed me by a good forty pounds or more, I ran right through them. I broke one guy's ribs and knocked a couple of teeth out of the other one. When I stepped into the ring for the final match, my opponent never showed up. He claimed to be injured or something and skipped out the back door.

I got my hand raised and a nice wad of cash in my pocket. I would have competed in future events, but soon after my victory the city of Redding shut Toughman down. I guess at one of the events a whole slew of Hell's Angels turned up to support their boy in the tournament, and when their boy lost a controversial decision, they incited a full-fledged riot. So, once again, it was back to the bars.

I tried to pull in cash wherever I could. I was working at the Premier Club in Reno, and every so often a group of male exotic dancers would come to the club to entertain the local women. I don't know how it happened, but one night when these dancers were in town, a couple of the women in the audience talked me into putting down my flashlight, hopping up on stage, and then taking off my clothes. I did pretty good, made a nice wad of one-dollar bills, so I decided to stick with it. From that point on, every time the dancers rolled into town, I'd hop up on stage. As you've probably guessed, I was desperate for money.

I was going nowhere in a hurry. In addition to pealing my clothes off to make a couple of extra bucks, I was also beginning to party more and more. I'd stay out too late, pour down too many beers, get into too many fights, and then wake up the next afternoon and start all over again. I still had the goal of becoming a professional football player, but I realized if I waited around for that to happen I might be too fat or drunk to play. What I needed was something to identify with, a job that could make me feel a part of something. I didn't want to be sitting behind a desk or pumping insecticide under somebody's house. I needed a job that would make me feel proud, so I decided to join the Marine Corps.

When I broke the news to my father, he was irate. He'd spent nearly a decade trying to get rid of my anger. He'd spent countless hours by my side when I felt as if I were going to explode with rage. He'd gotten me into football and wrestling, drove me to every game. After all those years getting me to a point where I could function in society and live the life of a normal human being, he feared that the Marine Corps was going to revert me back to the bundle of rage I had been when the state dumped me on his doorstep.

"I don't want you to become a professional killer!" he shouted and then threw up his hands and stormed off.

He didn't talk to me for a week, but that didn't stop me from following through with my plans. In the summer of 1984 I went down to Camp Pendleton in San Diego to begin my basic training. I had heard that Marine boot camp was weeks and weeks of living hell, but I didn't find it all that hard. I blew through the physical training, which was their primary tool for breaking young soldiers down. What I did find hard, however, was not punching my superiors every time they got in my face. I mean, these guys got right up in my face, their spit pelting me in the eyes. And they were always barking orders—get down and give me twenty push-ups! Get down and give me a hundred sit-ups! I don't think any of them knew just how close they were to getting their jaw broken.

But I guess I did OK keeping my cool because they made me platoon leader. They placed my bunk up at the head of the barracks so I could watch over the sixty other recruits. At first I thought being in a position of authority was great because it meant that I was turning out to be a good soldier, but then came the late-night inspections. If someone in the barracks didn't shine their boots, the sergeant would flip my bed upside down. If someone forgot to make his bed, the sergeant would get in my face and let the spit fly. If someone forgot to put away his toothbrush, the sergeant made me do a hundred push-ups. There were over sixty men in that barrack, and at least one of them forgot to do something every single night.

I got my aggression out when we did hand-to-hand combat training. Instead of letting us beat on each other with our fists and feet, they gave us long sticks padded with foam and told us to go to town. As it turned out, I was just as talented with a pugil stick as I was with punches. I was knocking out guys left and right. I was shaping up to be quite a fine soldier, and my sergeants recognized that. They treated me different than most of the others. I was becoming somewhat of their poster boy, and I liked it.

Five weeks in, I knew that I was going to be a lifer. Just like my father expected, all that anger I had worked so hard to subdue came rushing back to the surface. I was already acquiring the mind-set that would allow me to kill. I wouldn't have necessarily liked some of the things that the Marine Corps would have made me do, but I would have been good at it. They could have dropped me in a swamp in some third world country, and I would have done my best to kill everyone in that swamp. I might not have made it out alive, but I would have died with honor. That's what my father had worried about. He knew me better than anyone, better than I knew myself sometimes. He understood the way I thought, the strange code that I lived by. He knew that the Marine Corps would turn me into a professional killer, and he was right.

Fortunately I didn't have the option of taking that road. Six weeks into my training, the Navy discovered that I had broken my neck in high school. I had given that bit of news to my recruiting officer, and he hadn't cared. Apparently, the Navy did. They wanted me out, but the Marine Corps didn't want to kick me out. Here they had this young soldier who was strong, could fight like a banshee, and was down for whatever they threw his way. It became quite a little battle to decide my fate. The Navy called my father to come down and pick me up, but he ended up staying in San Diego for two weeks because neither side was willing to budge. Eventually, however, the Navy won.

I was so devastated when I heard the news that I actually got a little teary-eyed. Some of my drill sergeants saw this, and they got in my face. As a kid, I had gotten teary-eyed often when someone got in my face, and I learned that the only way to keep my eyes from spilling over was to start throwing punches. And it worked wonders—the moment my first punch landed, my eyes would instantly dry. That was part of the reason why I'd gotten into so many fights. I hadn't had to worry about that in a long, long time, but now I found myself in a little bit of a pickle. I wasn't about

to let my sergeants see me cry, so I only had one option. I went crazy. I started by flipping over a desk, and then I went after everyone in the room. My drill sergeants had seen what I could do with a pugil stick, and none of them wanted to find out what I could do with my fists. They all went running out of the barracks and that was the end of my military career.

I was back to square one. I had no money, no job, and no direction. I began fighting in the nightclubs, on the street, anywhere. If someone was picking on someone I was with or someone I even vaguely knew, I would always get in the middle and be the first one to throw a blow. It didn't matter if that someone wanted to settle his own matters, I beat him to the punch. If a fight was going to happen, I wanted to be the one in the thick of battle. It was a temporary release for my pent-up frustrations, but I knew that if I kept it up, it was only a matter of time before I found myself locked behind bars. I needed to find a direction, and I needed to find it quick.

Not long after I got out of the military, I remember sitting next to the fireplace in my father's home, my head sunk down into my hands. My father was talking to me, trying to cheer me up, but I was pretty down in the dumps. Then he said seven words that struck a cord. He said, "You ought to be a professional wrestler."

I lifted my head out of my hands, thought about it.

"I don't know, pop, professional wrestling is fake."

My father took offense to that. It's not what I said, but rather how I said it. He'd been watching men fly from the top ropes since he was a kid. Back in the fifties, most households only had one television. My father, Bob, used to flip to the station that had pro wrestling. His father would then flip to a different channel, calling pro wrestling stupid and fake. My father would then flip the channel back, putting up a fight. He knew it was fake then, and he knew it was fake now. But that didn't stop him from loving the hell out of it.

I hadn't watched much professional wrestling at that point, and the little I had seen didn't seem all that appealing. But when my father told me how much money a professional wrestler could make, my ears perked up real quick. We got to talking about the sport, and by the end of our conversation I decided to give it a whirl. After all, how hard could fake wrestling be? If it could put some change in my pockets, I was all for it.

My father did some research and learned that "Mad Dog" Buzz Sawyer had a school down in Sacramento, which was just a couple-hour drive from our house in Susanville. I learned that Sawyer had been a big-time wrestler back when Rick Flare was really young. In 1982, he took fourth place in PWI's "Most Hated" Poll, and in 1983 he was beat out only by Roddy Piper and Hulk Hogan in the "Inspirational Wrestler of the Year" Poll. So my father was pretty jazzed about the opportunity for me to learn from him. I didn't expect much, and I expected even less when I walked through the doors of his school. There wasn't a big fancy ring like you see on TV, just a bunch of grungy mats spread out on the floor. There were no punching bags or weight-lifting equipment or jump ropes. I wasn't quite sure what a pro-wrestling gym should be equipped with, but whatever that was, this gym certainly didn't have it.

Then I met Buzz Sawyer the man, and things started to perk up a little bit. He was a big guy, pushing upwards of 260 pounds, and I learned that he was a NCAA champion at the time, which meant that

he could also do the real wrestling. So after a little talking, my father paid the $250 tryout fee, and Buzz and I climbed onto the mats. I was expecting that he would grab me in some sort of headlock and then grunt and groan as if he were really putting it on. Then we would switch rolls and I would get to see how well I could grunt and groan. That didn't happen. What did happen was Buzz came at me with power and speed, trying to put the hurt on young Kenneth. As I have already mentioned, I hadn't seen much professional wrestling, but I had seen enough to know this certainly wasn't it. Buzz wanted to wrestle for real, which suited me just fine.

At the time I had no idea that Buzz had a scam going on, and that I was intended to be the next victim of this scam. I guess he'd advertised his school all over the place, seeking out men young and old who'd always dreamed of learning how to fly off the top ropes from a real-deal guy like Buzz. I don't know what Buzz promised them when they called for further information, but he managed to get a lot of guys to show up. He'd collect their $250 nonrefundable tryout free at the door and then send them onto the grungy mats he had thrown down on the floor. Instead of showing them classic wrestling moves, Buzz twisted and wrenched on their limbs for the next thirty minutes straight. He slapped on holds that you would never ever see in a professional wrestling match, holds that caused a great deal of pain. By the time he was through, the guys who had come with such high hopes wanted nothing more to do with professional wrestling. They walked out the door without the slightest complaint about their $250 and were never seen again.

When I climbed onto the mats with good old

Buzz, he thought I was just another one of those guys. But a few minutes after we put our paws on each other, he realized I wasn't. I hadn't wrestled since high school, and I only weighed 215 pounds or so, but I made Buzz pay. If what we had been doing was actually professional wrestling, then I think Buzz would have thrown in the towel right then and there. I worked him over pretty damn good.

His scam had come back to bite him in the ass, but being the man that he was, he wasn't about to give it up. He let me keep my $250, and he said that I had passed the tryout and was now a part of his school. I knew something fishy was going on, but I just thought that was the way the business worked. You had to prove that you were tough before anyone was going to hand over any secrets. So I came back the following week.

This time, however, I wasn't alone. There were several other guys lined up around the mats, all with $250 in their hands. Buzz collected their money, and then he told them to climb onto the mats with me to get their introduction to the world of professional wrestling. If they could pass the tryout, then they were in.

I hadn't learned a single professional wrestling move, so I did what I knew how to do, which was wrestle for real. The first guy I went up against weighed nearly 270 pounds. He was a college football player who looked meaner than hell. With all the other candidates standing around watching, I shot for his legs, took him to the ground, and bloodied his nose with a solid cross-face. Then I let him back up and shot in again, throwing in another cross-face and causing more blood to spill. After working this big, burly football player over for ten

minutes, all the other guys standing around watching approached Buzz and asked for their money back. Buzz, puffing out his barrel chest, kindly informed them that there were no refunds. They could climb onto the mat with me and attempt to pass the tryout or they could scuttle their butts straight out the door. They all scuttled their butts straight out the door.

At the end of the day, Buzz told me that I had done a great job, that we would begin my professional wrestling education as soon as he got his school off the ground. Then he handed me fifty bucks and told me to come back the following week.

I came back the following week, and then the week after that. I don't know how Buzz did it, but each week there was a new group of men lined up around the grungy mats on the floor with $250 in their hands. They all had to fill out a questionnaire before they were allowed inside, and if they were going through college, working in nightclubs, or just scraping by, I would beat them up. But if they had good jobs or Buzz knew they had money tucked away, they would be taken on as "students." I remember this one guy came in who had his own plumbing company, and Buzz convinced him to cough up a big chunk of cash up front to get him into the business. Eventually the guy started wondering why he wasn't learning any moves or getting his career off the ground as promised, so Buzz brought him over to Japan to do a match with him. A couple minutes into the match, however, Buzz did a power bomb with him off the top rope and broke the guy's neck.

After nearly a year helping line Buzz's pocketbook, my father realized Buzz had no plans of coaching me on professional wrestling. I hadn't yet stepped into a ring, and other than a few hammerlocks, I hadn't learned a single professional wrestling hold. Although I still hadn't the slightest clue what professional wrestling was all about, I had it set in my mind that I was going to be a professional wrestler.

While my father did some more research to find me a legitimate school, I lived up the Reno nightlife. Sometime during this partying spree I learned that the wrestling trials for the 1988 Olympics were coming to town, and I signed up. Then I forgot about it. A few weeks later I was coming home from the bars with a friend of mine, Lance Hill, and I remembered that the trials were that day. The sun was just coming up. Both of us were still drunk, and neither one of us had slept. We didn't feel like calling it a night yet, so we headed over to the gymnasium to see how I could fare against the world's best wrestlers after an all-night drinking binge.

A half hour later I was sitting on the wrestling mats with a bunch of other young men who had trained all their life for this moment. They had spent years bleeding, sweating, and pouring out their hearts every day during training just to get a shot at the Olympics. You could see the determination in their eyes as they taped their broken fingers and stretched their limbs in preparation for battle. And here I was, sitting off in a corner trying to conceal my booze breath and focus my vision. I had no idea it was going to be so serious. If I had, I might have taken the time to do a little research. I might have even discovered that freestyle wrestling, which is what they did in the Olympics, was nothing like high school wrestling, which was all I knew. I thought wrestling was wrestling.

I learned that that wasn't the case when I climbed onto the mats with a muscle-bound kid from Syracuse, New York. We started going at it, and then all of a sudden he starts racking up points in three-increment blocks for doing these silly little turns. The more points that he racked up, the angrier I got. Eventually I realized that there was no way I was going to beat this kid on points, not with this lame scoring system they had in place, so I flipped him over to his back and pinned him. One, two, three—you're out.

I walked off the mats still grumbling about the rules, but I decided to hang around and see if I could take it all the way. Not understanding how to score points, however, did me in. The coach came over to me before I left and gave me some words of encouragement. He said that if I'd trained in freestyle wrestling, as all the other boys had, I would have gone to the Olympics. He suggested that I get the training that I needed, and then come back in four years. I might have followed his suggestion if I hadn't already made up my mind to do an entirely different kind of wrestling.

Not long after the trials, my father told me that he had discovered a legitimate school out in North Carolina run by Nelson Royal and Gene Anderson, two legitimate wrestlers. Both of us were excited, but we also knew it would require some pretty big sacrifices. I had married the previous year, and my son Ryan was on the way. My father would have to sell his home. But after getting together and talking about it, it sounded like the best move to make, even though everything about it was so uncertain. Just a few months before we were supposed to leave, I got an invitation from the San Diego Chargers to come down and try out for the team, but my sights were already locked. The family was headed to North Carolina.

2

Off the Ropes

THERE WAS ANOTHER TRYOUT AWAITING ME IN
North Carolina, but this one was legitimate. And I
smoked it. Nelson Royal had the group of us young
hopefuls start off with an hour of push-ups, sit-ups,
and sprints. Then he tossed us into the ring one by
one to see how we faired against the four burly professional wrestlers that had turned up. They had us
doing amateur wrestling, so I was OK. Actually, I was
better than OK. I worked them over just like I had
worked over Buzz Sawyer. Out of the entire group, I
was the only one to pass the tryout and get admitted
to the school.

At the end of the day, my father forked over an
ungodly amount, something like six thousand dollars, and I began my schooling in the art of professional wrestling. While the family was getting
acquainted with our new home in Mooresville, North
Carolina, I was learning how to fly off the top ropes
and slap on submission holds that looked like they
hurt but didn't. I had been told that it usually took
anywhere between fifteen months and two years to
complete the training, but professional wrestling
came natural to me, as had both football and amateur
wrestling. I was able to anticipate my opponent's
moves, and I'd had enough of a background in real
fighting to make the holds look real. Within four

months, I had completed my training
and was ready to hit the road.

As it turned out, I hit the sky instead. Only days
after receiving my professional wrestling diploma, I
found myself on a plane headed for the Land of the
Rising Sun to do a thirty-day tour for Old Japan,
Japan's number one professional wrestling organization at the time. It was a rough thirty days. First off,
I was as green as could be, wrestling some experienced veterans—Dug Vernus, Danny Crawford, the
Can-Am Connection boys. Their professional
wrestling was a lot faster than I was used to. I had a
hard time figuring out their movement, and I
couldn't seem to remember the spots. I quickly got
lost in the shuffle and fell behind, so I had to spend
several hours in the ring before each match just to
get myself prepared.

And when it came time to wrestle in front of the
crowd, I kept feeling like I was blowing it. The only
professional wrestling I had seen was in the United
States, and the crowd always went nuts. Even when
the matches were absolutely horrible, the crowd
went nuts. When I stepped into the ring in Japan,
you could hear a pin drop. Every once in a while you
would get an "Ooooo" or an "Aaaaa" out of them,
but for the most part, silence. It wasn't until I had

been there for a while that I realized that they weren't any more silent for my matches than they were for everyone else's. That's just how they were. They were trying to show respect, and once I learned that, I loved them for it.

I didn't, however, love their cuisine. Even though sushi is one of my favorite things to eat now, it made me gag back then. I was on a constant search for a steak house, and when I finally found one—it was called Roberto's Steak House—I discovered that a steak cost forty dollars. I didn't get a whole lot of money for food, so I had to ration out the steaks. A lot of the guys who had spent some time wrestling in Japan had gotten used to the food. While they were slurping down gooey fish and slimy things you couldn't even identify, I was twiddling my thumbs and salivating in anticipation of my next streak, which always seemed to be three days away.

Getting from one arena to the next also wasn't easy. We had twelve big wrestlers packed onto a very small bus. We'd drive four hours to our destination, shuffle off the bus, head into the arena to wrestle, and then head back to a hotel that had no resemblance to the kind of hotels I was used to. They were the size of a matchbox. Every time I tried to roll over in bed, I'd end up falling out and banging my head on the toilet. The only time I didn't fall out of bed and bang my head on the toilet was in a hotel that didn't have toilets in the room. They only had one bathroom per floor, and it can be a pretty gruesome sight heading into a shower after eleven other professional wrestlers have already gotten their wash on.

Needless to say, I didn't take to Japan that first time I went over. A part of it had to do with the fact that I was uncomfortable because I was still so green,

feeling like I wasn't pulling my weight in the ring. A part of it had to do with the fact that I wasn't yet accustomed to life on the road. But it's amazing how a little time and experience can change a man. Now Japan is one of my favorite places in the world, full of colorful people and places. My first time over there, I guess I was just so consumed with trying to find my niche that it was hard to truly open my eyes to all that was going on around me.

When I stepped off the plane in Charlotte, North Carolina, I was happy to see my family. I was also eager to start wrestling in the good old U.S. of A. I had gotten all the kinks in my game straightened out over in Japan, and, thanks to Gene Anderson and Nelson Royal, I had gotten a gig with the South Atlantic Professional Wrestling Association (SAPW) on the East Coast. So, my father and I hit the road.

We traveled to Winston-Salem, Wilkesboro, Columbia, Atlanta, and a dozen other cities in the southeast. Sometimes I'd perform in front of fifty people in a high school gym or a veteran's war memorial building. Other times I would entertain hundreds of people in the Winston-Salem Coliseum or the Memorial Coliseum in Charlotte. And then sometimes the show got canceled because only seven spectators turned up. The only thing constant was the money—no matter how big the show, I usually only made enough to pay for the gas back home. Technically we were in a rough spot, but that's not where our heads were. We had moved east to fulfill a dream, and now we were living it. There was no doubt in my mind that as long as I stuck with it, I would make it to the top.

And besides, I had never seen my father so happy. Every Friday and Saturday night we would be on the road, heading to some new destination. One of his favorite things in this world is to drive, so he would stay up all night behind the wheel while I napped in the passenger's seat. And when we got to an event, my father would jump into the mix and help the promoters set up the ring. He'd work his way around the crowd, find someone interesting, and have an hour-long conversation about professional wrestling. He was truly in the height of his glory, living out a fantasy he'd had since his childhood. Both of us were having a blast.

It wasn't long until I started seeing the same faces in different towns, and I realized that people were actually making a two- or three-hour drive just to see me perform. The fans made me feel accomplished; they made me feel like I was actually going someplace. I wouldn't have turned my back on a single one of them, but it did start getting a little hard for my family. At that time, many of the fans were convinced that professional wrestling was real. They bought every line and gimmick hook-line-and-sinker. If I did or said something that they didn't agree with, they opened up the phone book. They all knew that I wrestled out of Charlotte, and with there only being one Shamrock in the Charlotte phone book, it didn't take them long to find my number. Then they'd called me up to give me a piece of their mind. My wife usually answered the phone.

It didn't take long before my family got tired of the angry phone calls, so I stopped using my real name and started going by Vince Tortelli. I don't recall how the name came about, but I kept it because people thought it fit my Italian look. The name change didn't affect my popularity in the slightest. I was drawing larger crowds at every show, performing in cities further away each week. But

despite my accomplishments in the ring, professional wrestling still wasn't paying the bills.

With my father doing a majority of the bread earning working at a local group home, I started scouring the city for illegal prizefights. I was surprised by how many I could find. I fought in the backrooms of bars and in vacant parking lots. Seldom did I walk away with more than fifty bucks in my pocket, but every little bit counted.

Just as money started to really get tight, I heard about a Toughman competition they were having in Statesville, which was close to our home. Ever since I had won the money at the Redding Toughman contest, I had been keeping my eye out for them. There had been a couple of shows on the East Coast, but most of them had been a six- or seven-hour drive away from where we lived, and we didn't want to waste the money on gas. But now that they had one in Statesville, I wasn't going to pass up on the opportunity to make some easy money. And for the most part it was easy money. I blew through the competitors and took home close to a thousand dollars. That was more money than I made in several months doing professional wrestling, so when I heard that they were having another contest in Hickory, which was also close to our home, I went down there and entered it.

The purse for the winner of this tournament was $2,500. I went through my first two competitors with ease, but when I stepped into the finals the following day, I found myself up against a guy with over fifty armature fights. Seconds into the first round, he stepped forward and hit me with a six- or seven-punch combination. At that point, I still hadn't learned any boxing skills. I knew enough about the sweet science, however, to realize that if I tried to get fancy, I would probably end up lying on the canvas with the whites of my eyes showing. So I did what came naturally—I started to brawl. I powered into him and hit him with these big sledgehammer fists. At one point, I even pushed him out of the ring. It was a tough back-and-forth battle, but in the end my street fighting experience put me over the top and dropped $2,500 in my pocket.

Before I could skip out to the parking lot, the promoter caught up to me. I knew something had been a little fishy in that last fight, and he confirmed my suspicions.

"Man," he said, shaking his head, "you just beat my ringer."

Most promoters were not in the habit of sharing the fact that they had a ringer in their tournament, but I could tell this guy was busted up over having lost $2,500. If the promoter's ringer had won, the promoter would have only had to pay him what they'd agreed upon ahead of time, which, from the look on his face, was a lot less than $2,500. I figured that the only reason the promoter told me about the ringer was that he wanted me to become the new ringer. I wasn't interested, not after doing a year of Buzz Sawyer's dirty work, so I turned and walked away.

That decision came back to haunt me. I was getting the idea that I was pretty good at this Toughman thing, so whenever a tournament came around, I started to rely on the money before stepping into the ring. And it was a lot of money to count on. In my last competition, I had made more money in one night that I did in a year wrestling on the road. Well, I heard that they were having a tournament up in Charlotte for all the guys who had already won an

event. It was sort of like the Ultimate Ultimate would be—everyone wanted to know who the toughest Toughman fighter was. I had already won two events, so I naturally thought that they would let me compete. I was wrong. They banned me from the event, and when I asked them why they had banned me, they said it was because I was too tough. Right then I knew what had happened. They had found another ringer, and this time they wanted to be sure that I didn't go in there and beat him.

I didn't spend too much time worrying about it because things were starting to happen for me in the world of professional wrestling. My name, Vince Tortelli, was starting to get around, and I got a chance to do a couple of house shows in Salem, Massachusetts, for the World Wrestling Federation (WWF). It was a pretty big deal. Most professional wrestlers wait years and years for such an opportunity. Some wait all of their life. So it was something that I took very seriously. I trained hard in preparation, determined to prove that I had what it took to entertain the masses.

And I think I did that in my first couple of matches. I was paired up with Barry Horowitz, a great worker who had been around a long, long time. He understood that professional wrestling was more than just a bunch of random moves and then a finish. He knew how to build a story around a match, create drama that the fans could identify with, and that's exactly what we did. I walked away from our bouts feeling accomplished and satisfied. I felt like I had done a good job, and that's all that really mattered to me because whether I got into the WWF or not was not something I could control.

Then they asked me back, and I got excited. I had passed the first stage of the tryout, and this was the second stage. I didn't know how many stages there were, but I didn't care. My goal was to reach the top, and I was currently taking the steps needed to get there. But instead of paring me up with Horowitz, who had made me look so damn good during my debut, they paired me up with Tom McGee. They called him "Mega Man," but I had no idea why. He wasn't Mega in anything he did. It's not that he didn't have any moves. He had plenty of moves. He just didn't want or know how to string those moves together in a way that would build up the match. It's not like you had to be a brain surgeon to be able to do that. He could have come out and socked me in the face, kicked me in the gut, and then picked me up and slammed me to the ground. While I rolled around in agony, he could have caught me in a painful hold and twisted my head. I would have kicked my feet, convulsed my body. Then, just before the ref pounded his hand for the third time on the canvas, I would have escaped. That would have built the match a little, got the fans riled up, but instead it was, "Hey, let's just do these moves and we're done." He just wanted to go spot after spot after spot, and then "boom," the finish.

I did two matches with him, and both of them turned out absolutely horrible. I remember coming backstage after our second bout completely depressed. I was still relatively green, still trying to get a foothold in the business, and I thought the lack of build had been my fault. While I was sulking, one of the Anderson brothers came up and tapped on my shoulder.

"Don't worry about it," he said. "It wasn't you. That guy has a horrible match with everybody."

It made me feel a little better, but it didn't do any wonders for getting me into the WWF. After that last show with Mega Man, I didn't hear back from them, so I continued wrestling for the SAPW on the East Coast. I figured if I made a big enough impact on the smaller circuits, then it was only a matter of time before the WWF gave me another chance.

I started to get to know more people and make more friends in the business. Every time one of those friends came through town on their circuit, my pop and I would put him up for a couple of nights so he didn't have to stay in a hotel. Professional wrestlers are generally not the kind of men who like to sit around watching television, so we would go out and get some drinks. The problem was we almost always had someone over, so I was going out and getting drinks more often than my family or I liked. It was only a matter of time before I got into some kind of trouble.

As it turned out, that trouble started over a girl.

I was sitting up at the bar of a local dive with a friend of mine who wrestled on some of the smaller circuits. He and his girlfriend were in town for a few days, and naturally I had taken them out for a couple of drinks to show them some fun. As we were sitting there, the Nasty Boys came sauntering in. They were wrestling for the WWF at the time, and I guess they thought that gave them special privileges because the blond one, I believe his name is Knobs, came up to the bar and grabbed the chest of my buddy's girlfriend.

She got mad, of course. I could tell my buddy wanted to come to her rescue, but he wasn't much of a fighter. Besides, the Nasty Boys were with the WWF, and my buddy was desperately trying to get into the WWF. He didn't want to stir up any unnecessary waves, so he let her handle it. And she seemed to be doing a pretty good job of it, too.

But then Knobs reached forward and pinched her chest again. My buddy spun around on his bar stool, but he managed to keep his cool. He said only three words—"Dude, come on."

Back in the day I probably would have already been throwing punches, but I was trying to get away from stepping into the middle of every fight that happened. I had children now, and the last thing I needed was another lawsuit for hurting someone in public. I tried my hardest just to stay in my seat and drink my drink, but the moment Knobs laid his hands on my friend, all that anger and rage came bubbling back up to the surface.

"You know what," I said to Knobs, standing up, "You better back up."

I was still hoping that there would be some sort of peaceful resolution. I knew the Nasty Boys weren't going to say they were sorry and buy my friend's girlfriend a drink, but I was hoping they'd fire off a few nasty words and then skip out the door.

That didn't happen. What did happen was Knobs put his hand on my face and shoved me back. I think he saw the change in my facial expression the moment he did that because he didn't wait around for a response. By the time I could get my weight moving in a forward direction, both of them were already headed for the door. I was so mad that I would probably have caught them even though they had a good head start, but the bouncers intercepted me halfway across the floor.

"Come on, Ken, chill, chill, chill."

When they let go of me, both of the Nasty Boys were long gone. The smart thing would have been to let it go, but that's not something I could do. I had learned at five years of age what mattered most in my life. It wasn't looks or money or health. It was my pride. The Nasty Boys had picked a fight with us. They had disrespected my friend's girlfriend, then my friend, and then they had disrespected me. If I didn't settle the score, they would walk away thinking I was a chump, and I couldn't have that. The only thought circling around in my mind was *I'm not going to let this happen!*

I knew the hotel the Nasty Boys were staying in, so after I said goodnight to my friend and his girl-friend, I headed over there. I banged on their door for a good five minutes, and when they wouldn't open it, I kicked the door down. As I stormed into their room, I saw Knobs lying on the bed. He looked passed out, and I started kicking the side of the bed to wake him up to fight me.

"Get up!" I shouted.

I remember seeing Knobs stir on the bed, and then my world went black. When I woke up an hour or so later, I was lying in the back of an ambulance. I had a broken sternum, and my eye socket was caved in. I was in such bad shape that the paramedics thought they were going to lose me before they could get me to the hospital. I looked like someone had run me over with a tractor several dozen times.

While recovering in the hospital over the next couple of months, I learned what had happened that night. I guess when I was beating on their door, the Nasty Boys realized that there was no way they were going to be able to stop me from getting into their room, so they worked up a little scheme. Knobs lay down in bed and pretended to be passed out, and his partner in crime, Saggs, ripped the phone out of the wall and hid in the closet. Now, I don't know what kind of hotel this was, but they didn't have your run-of-the-mill phone. Instead of being constructed primarily out of plastic, this one was constructed primarily out of steel. As I was preoccupied with kicking the bed in an attempt to wake Knobs up, Saggs came up behind me with that god-awful phone. He swung it over his shoulder with all of his might, hitting me upside the head and knocking me out cold.

It was a scenario you might see acted out in the WWE on *Monday Night Raw*, and they carried it just as far. Once I was down, they started tap dancing on my face and ribs and legs with their steal-toed boots. Then, after kicking me several hundred times, they decided to go for the grand finale. They dragged my body out the front door and tried dumping me over the balcony. The commotion had awakened some of the other wrestlers staying in the hotel, and when they saw that the Nasty Boys were trying to dump my limp body three stories onto the cement parking lot, they quickly intervened. A few minutes later, an ambulance arrived and carted me away.

It took several months to heal, and in that time my hatred for the Nasty Boys grew. I had no intentions of letting this matter fly by the wayside. It wasn't one of those times where the protagonist of the story comes to some earth-shattering revelation while lying in bed, learns a valuable lesson about life, and then finds peace with everything that happened. No, I was most definitely going to get revenge. I knew it was only a matter of time before I ran into the Nasty Boys again, and then we would settle our differences ourselves. No cops, no lawyers. Just the three of us.

And when I got that revenge, which you will learn about soon enough, it was just as sweet as I had imagined it.

3

Land of the Rising Sun

ONCE MY BROKEN BONES HEALED UP, I WASTED little time getting back into the ring. Not long after my return, Dean Malenko, a wrestler known as "The Man with a Thousand Holds," approached me at one of the shows. I had done some wrestling with his brother, Joe Malenko, over in Japan. Dean and I started talking, and I learned that he was going to be in town for a couple of months, so I invited him to stay at my house so he wouldn't have to rent an apartment. He had spent a considerable amount of time wrestling over in Japan, and one afternoon he pulls out a videotape of the matches going on over there in the Union of Wrestling Forces (UWF). I didn't have the best time while I was over in Japan, so I hadn't paid much attention to their wrestling organizations after I left. This videotape, however, completely blew me away. It didn't look like they were wrestling; it looked like they were fighting. The match that I found particularly intriguing was Masakatsu Funaki vs. Minoru Suzuki, two famous Japanese professional wrestlers. It was strictly a submission wrestling match, no kicks or punches allowed, but these guys were going at it. It was super fast paced. They were shooting for each other's legs, dumping each other on their backs, and wrenching on each other's limbs with submission holds. Everything they did was technical

and precise. I thought it was real—and, in many ways, it was real. They were using real techniques that could cause pain, but they weren't locking them down. It was a "work," which meant that it was fake, but it looked a whole lot like a "shoot," which was a real fight.

By the time the match was over, I was speechless. It was just like the first time I saw a football game—I knew that was what I wanted to do, and I also knew that I would be good at it.

Dean and I kept in touch when he went back home to Florida. I even flew down there a couple of times to do some matches with him. Then one day he gives me a call and tells me that Masami "Sammy" Saranaka, the man who did the majority of the recruiting for the UWF, was coming to town to visit his father, who was a big time wrestler from the 1970s. Dean had talked it over with Saranaka, and they had arranged a little tryout for me down in Florida to see if I had what it took to compete in the UWF.

Tryouts have always been my strong suit, and this time was no different. They threw a bunch of guys into the ring with me, and I beat them with my strength and wrestling ability. I didn't know any submissions at that point; I just shot for their legs, dumped them to the ground, and then manhandled them. I wasn't as technical as they were, but I was in such good shape they couldn't touch me. I passed the tryout with flying colors.

I might have been a decent professional wrestler at that point, but when it came to submission wrestling, I was still green. To get the preliminary training that I needed, I spent the next two months flying back and forth between North Carolina and Florida. I'd train for a couple of days, absorb as much as I could, and then fly back home. I definitely felt like I was starting to get a grasp on some of the different holds and locks, but submission wrestling is not something that you can master in a couple of months, especially if you only train a couple of times a week. I would have liked another couple of months to get a handle on all the basic positions, but as it turned out, I had another tryout waiting for me over in Japan. So, still as green as can be, I found myself on a plane headed back to the Land of the Rising Sun.

The moment I stepped into the UWF dojo in Tokyo, I knew this was going to be like no tryout I had gone through before. The place was spotless, as clean as a whistle, but you could still smell the sweat and blood that had spilled in the joint over the years. I was nervous, but in a good way. I was eager to show them that I had what it took. I realized that for the first time in a long time, someone might actually push me past my physical and mental limits, and that excited me.

The first guy they had me grapple had the title of "young boy," which meant that he was still in training. He was a tough kid, but he was no match for my strength. We went for a half hour straight, and I handled him. Then they stuck me with another young boy, Takaku Fuke. He wasn't as tough a fighter back then as he is now, but he was still tough. We went for a half hour straight, and I handled him.

I wasn't gassed out, but I was pretty damn tired. An hour straight of hard grappling is no walk in the park, let me tell you. So I'm sitting there, trying to catch my breath, and then Minoru Suzuki, one of the men that I had seen do incredible things on Dean's videotape, pulled me down onto the mats. We went for a half hour straight, and he handled the hell out of me. I got caught in arm bars, chokes, heel hooks—I got caught in submissions I didn't even know existed. And when Suzuki was done with me, I had to go another half hour with Funaki, the other amazing submission wrestler I had seen in the videotape. He'd catch me in a hold, I'd struggle to free myself, and then he'd apply pressure until I writhed in pain and tapped my hand in submission.

The upper body holds weren't that bad because I could use my strength to muscle out of a lot of them. But the leg locks killed me. I had no idea how to defend against them. In today's MMA competition, most people know how to escape leg locks, but back then they were the craftiest submission out there. When I got caught in one, I had two choices—tap or get my leg broken. It made a powerful impression on me, and that's the reason why I became such a leg tactician. In all the brawls I had been in throughout my life, never once had I thought about attacking my opponent's legs or looking out for my opponent trying to attack mine. I figured most people were like that, and it left them vulnerable. It didn't matter how big or strong or fast they were; if I could isolate one of their legs, I could win the fight.

By the time Suzuki and Funaki were through with me, there was no question about it—I had gotten my ass handed to me. Other than having a phone slammed into the back of my head, it was the first time I had gotten beat up since I was a kid. If the try-out had been in the United States, in my backyard, I would have found some way to beat them down. But I was in their backyard, and they were there to help me. I didn't take the loss as a blow to my ego, I took it for what it was—a way for them to see what I was made of. And the only way for someone to know what you are made of, truly made of, is to break you down to the point where you can no longer stand, no longer fight, and yet you do.

I had done that, and after two hours of hell, they told me that I was in.

My education began the very next day at ten o'clock in the morning. We went for a run, lifted some weights, and then dove into hard grappling. At noon we all sat down and ate a dish called Chuckle, which was a mixture of rice, beef, and vegetables, from a massive pot. While digesting, we watched videotapes of matches and broke down the moves. A couple of the guys spoke a few words of English, but there was never small talk. If they said anything at all, it concerned training. Then, when our food had settled, we got off our butts and dove right back into hardcore grappling until the sun went down.

I pushed myself hard during these workouts. I was eager to learn, but I also had a lot of pressure on my shoulders. Funaki had scheduled my first match for only seven days after I had passed the tryout. In addition to having to learn all the holds and posi-tions, I also had to learn the rules of their organiza-tion. It wasn't like professional wrestling in the States. There was a red corner and a blue corner, and each corner had a board above it to keep track of the number of knockdowns. For a fifteen-minute fight,

they had a three-knockdown rule. If your opponent dropped you with punches or kicks and the ref gave you a count, it was considered a knockdown. If your opponent caught you in a submission hold and you were able to grab the rope, the ref would break you apart, but it would be counted as a knockdown. If you got three knockdowns marked on your board before you could put your opponent away, you lost the fight.

There was a lot to take in, but I felt confident that I could now do enough in the ring not to look like a complete amateur. And if I messed up once or twice, it wouldn't be that big of a deal. There was no way the organization was going to stick me into one of their bigger shows on my first night. I figured before I got a break I would have to prove myself, slowly climb the ladder like I had in the SAPW.

It wasn't until I walked down the runway and past the aisles of fans that I realized I had been wrong. Up to that point, I considered a large crowd to be anywhere between one hundred and two hun-dred people. That night there were seventeen thou-sand fans in attendance. I had never dreamed of per-forming in front of so many people, and it made me realize the popularity of the UWF. Although they had only been around a couple of years, they were selling out forty-thousand-seat arenas. The submission wrestling stuff was still new, but the whole country was going crazy for it.

Surprisingly, I wasn't nervous in the least. I had worked out on several occasions with my opponent, Yoji Anjo, and I knew that he was a good practi-tioner. I wasn't going to go in there and try to take his head off with a punch or kick, and he wasn't going to break my leg with a submission hold. If he caught me in a hold, I was going to fight it, sell it, and then slowly work my way to the ropes so I could get an escape. We were going to go at it, turn on the juice, but we weren't going to hurt each other.

It was my most memorable fight, even though it wasn't a real fight. I was young and green; yet the match flowed surprisingly well. I let Anjo beat on me with punches and kicks, and I wouldn't sell his strikes unless they landed. A few of the shots that he hit me with probably would have knocked many people out, but I have a hard head. I purposely took them to the face and jaw because I wanted this match to be the best match ever. And we went wild in the ring. Every time we got a reversal or a rope escape, the crowd would boom out with their "Oooos" and "Aaaas." Let me tell you, with seventeen thousand people in attendance, those were some loud "Oooos" and "Aaaas." I could feel them in my chest, and it filled me with a sense of accomplishment.

That satisfaction continued to grow when I won the bout and got my hand hefted into the air. It was the first time I had done anything like this, the first time I had competed in the UWF, but the crowd started chanting my name. I looked out into the rows of seats for the first time since I climbed into the ring, and I could see seventeen thousand faces staring at me, praising me for what I had just done. For the first time in a long time, I felt like I was exactly where I needed to be.

"This is awesome," I muttered under my breath.

After the match, people came up to me right and left. They all wondered if I was OK. The UWF wasn't like WWF—everyone thought it was real. They all thought I had been knocked out a couple times during the match, and they wanted to know if I was going to the hospital. Still selling it, of course, I told

them I was probably just going back to my hotel to get some rest. If I didn't feel better in the morning, then maybe I would go to the hospital.

In addition to making an impression with the fans, I also made an impression with the promoters. A month after my first match, they gave me a match with Funaki, my instructor. He was the king of the hill when it came to professional wrestling in Japan, and he was also the best submission wrestler out there. When we stepped into the ring together, it was a knock-down, drag-out, grappling match. We pushed each other to the limit for twelve minutes straight. It had already been determined that he was going to win the match, but when he tried to pick me up and slam me down for the finish, he toppled over because he was totally out of gas. Despite the anticlimactic ending, the fans appreciated how we had laid everything on the line. Even though I had lost, that fight brought me to instant stardom over in Japan.

Never had I been so fulfilled in life. I was in the gym every day, learning countless ways to defeat my opponents with submission holds. I was making good money, $1,200 a bout, which was a huge step up from what I was used to. And I started to fall in love with Japan. The food began to taste better, and although everything was just as cramped as it had been on my first visit, I seemed to fit in fine wherever I went. I had finally found the niche I had been looking for in my life. It seemed too good to be true, and then I realized that it was. Not long after my fight with Funaki, the UWF broke up.

I guess they were having trouble in the head office. Several of the better-known wrestlers started their own spin-off companies. There was the UWFI, RINGS, and Fujiwara-Gumi, which was run by

Yoshiaki Fujiwara. I had gotten pretty popular after my match with Funaki, and each of the organizations wanted me to go with them. I liked them all, and I would have been happy working for any one of them, but I decided to go with Fujiwara-Gumi because Fujiwara was friends with Sammy Saranaka, and Saranaka's family had given me my start. I also wanted to go where Funaki went. I was loyal to him because he was my teacher, but I also knew that he would push for more realistic bouts.

The day I signed the contract with Fujiwara, Saranaka came into my hotel room and dumped thirty thousand dollars onto my bed. The bills were bundled into ten-thousand-dollar stacks, and there were three stacks! I had never seen so much money at one time in my life. I thought I was rich. I was rich; at least for a little while. Thirty thousand dollars is a lot of money to have sitting in front of you, but it's not a lot of money when you have to ration it out for a whole year. Six months later it was all gone, and I still had another six months on my contract. Yeah, I learned a lesson with that one.

At the time, however, I couldn't have been happier. I would stay in Japan for a month and wrestle all day, every day. I became a human sponge, absorbing techniques from everyone. Sometimes I stayed in a hotel, other times I'd sleep in the dojo. Then I'd do a match and fly back home for a month. A month later, I'd fly back to Japan, do another match, and then stay until my next match. It was a pretty good system—I got to learn the art of submission fighting as well as see my family.

In just a matter of months, once Fujiwara brought his company up, I was the top dog in Japan. There were Ken Shamrock T-shirts and Ken

Shamrock phone cards. I was doing so well the organization started to bring in other foreigners to try to see if they could have the same success. I remember one time Saranaka brought over Dwayne Kowalski, a Greco-Roman wrestler on the U.S. Olympic Team. We were going to do a match together, so we got together in the dojo to work out the details. He was a phenomenal athlete, accustomed to manhandling everyone on the mat, so when it came down to deciding who was going to win our match, he made it clear that he didn't want to "put me over," which meant that he didn't want to let me win.

I knew exactly where he was coming from. He was just like me in that he hated to lose. It wasn't going to be a real loss, but the people in the audience weren't going to know that. If it started to get around in the amateur wrestling world that a professional wrestler had beaten him, he would never hear the end of it. And that's what he considered me, a professional wrestler. He had never before done submission wrestling, and I didn't feel he took it all that seriously. After all, he was a world-class Greco-Roman wrestler.

Kowalski didn't want to lose, nor did I want to lose. As we were trying to work out this detail, Saranaka came up with a solution. He suggested that we both climb into the ring and fight for real right there and then.

"Whoever wins goes over," Saranaka said, meaning whoever won the real fight would also get to win the fake one.

Kowalski was all for it. He wasn't gloating like he had already won, but I could tell that he was confident. He didn't think anyone could touch him on the wrestling mat.

"If you feel something painful, tap," Sammy told him, already knowing what the outcome would be.

With a nod of his head, Kowalski assumed his fighting stance in the ring. The moment we got the go-ahead to begin from Saranaka, I shot in on his legs, took him to the ground, and caught him in a heel hook. I forced him to tap.

"What the hell was that?" he asked, truly perplexed.

"A heel hook," I said.

"Well, I wasn't ready. I've been doing Greco, no one has shot in on me for years."

I agreed to give him another shot, so we climbed back into the ring. This time it took me twenty seconds to get him to the ground and catch him in a heel hook, and once I had it sunk, I put it on nice and tight just to let him know that I could break his leg. He still couldn't believe it, but he didn't demand another go. And when we stepped into the ring in front of twenty thousand fans a week later, he put me over without complaint. It went fairly well, too. Then, a short time after the match, I started coaching him in submission wrestling.

I was becoming an animal in the gym, learning hundreds of different ways to make an opponent scream in pain. I could catch my opponents all the time during practice, but I knew that was different than catching an opponent in a real fight. When two people are going at it with bad intentions, adrenaline is flowing; there's more at stake. A hold that worked in training might not have the same effect when your opponent's pride is riding on the line. I was Fujiwara's biggest star, wrestling in front of twenty-thousand people each month, but it was getting harder and harder for me to put my fellow wrestlers over. I didn't want to pull my punches and kicks. I

didn't want to release my submission holds once I had them sunk. I wanted to test out my newfound skills in actual battle.

Six months into my new career, I finally got that chance. At the time, there was a heated feud going on between the Japanese submission wrestlers and the Muay Thai kickboxers. For the past twenty years, the kickboxers had been widely regarded as the toughest fighters around; no one could touch them, but when the UWF had been in full swing, they claimed that their grapplers were tougher. The feud had never been resolved, so Fujiwara decided to give his organization a boost by capitalizing on the controversy. He called out Don Nakaya Nielson, the middleweight Muay Thai champion. Although Nakaya Nielson lived in Hawaii, he trained in Japan and was extremely popular. The bout was supposed to be worked, everything predetermined, but a few minutes into the bout, Nakaya Nielson threw a huge knee to Fujiwara's face and split him open.

Afterward, Fujiwara decided to settle the feud for real. There weren't, however, many submission wrestlers at the time that were willing to step into the ring with a Muay Thai kickboxer, especially one as experienced as Nakaya Nielson. They were hesitant because of all those knee and elbow strikes. There had never been a mixed martial arts competition before, at least not in Japan, so they didn't know how they would fare. They knew that submission wrestling was effective, they just didn't know how effective.

I had high expectations, so when Fujiwara asked me if I would fight with him, I said, "Yeah, sure, I'll do the fight." In addition to wanting to test my skills, I also wanted to get revenge for what Nakaya Nielson had done to Fujiwara.

The fight was put together, and then the press started. Nakaya Nielson talked all kinds of trash. He kept saying how he hoped that I had good insurance because when he was through with me, I was going to need it. He kept saying how he was going to put me in the hospital, over and over and over. The guy was like a broken record, and people were listening to what he had to say. He had been fighting a long, long time, and he was a trash-talking expert.

I, on the other hand, was still relatively green. I was young, and trash talking was definitely not my strong suit. I kept thinking, "What's with all the hostility, I don't even know this guy." So when the press came by asking what I thought about my opponent's comments, I just shrugged my shoulders and said, "I guess we will find out in the ring."

I still hadn't worked on any standup fighting at that point. Well, that's not entirely true. Back when I was fighting in the Toughman competitions on the East Coast, I had enrolled at a boxing gym and started taking lessons. My training had lasted a total of two weeks. They wanted me to reposition my stance, hold my hands in a different way. I was a brawler, and it worked for me. I figured that if I started changing everything I did, my game might fly right out the window.

I didn't feel the same way when training to fight Nakaya Nielson. I had started to realize the importance of learning how to strike efficiently and effectively, and I would get better and better at it as I got more heavily involved in MMA competition, but at the time I didn't feel like it made all that much difference. I knew Nakaya Nielson understood nothing about fighting on the ground, and once I brought him down into my world, he would be little more than putty in my hands. If he could keep the fight

standing, I might be in trouble, but I doubted very highly that he would be able to do that. This was back in the days when you were either a striker or a grappler, and although competitors from both disciplines had yet to converge in a ring to see how the different styles mixed, I had a hard time seeing how Nakaya Nielson would keep me from taking him to the ground with little to no takedown defense. I had managed to take Kowalski to the ground, and he had one of the best takedown defenses in the world. Nakaya Nielson might be able to catch me with a punch or a knee on my way in, but I had been hit with a lot of punches and knees. If he wanted to knock me out, he would have to hit me with more than one shot.

Because of my confidence, excitement was the only thing that I felt when I climbed into the ring with Don Nakaya Nielson on the night of the fight. Forty thousand fight fans had turned up to watch this first-of-its-kind battle, and it sent a chill down my spine. There was no fear, no hesitation. This was the moment I had been waiting for, a chance to test my skills in combat. A chance to prove myself in front of thousands of people. And to top it all off, I got to prove myself against a guy who'd gotten on my bad side by talking a whole bunch of trash.

We circled each other in the center of the ring for a moment, and when he didn't go for anything, I threw a couple of jabs as bait. They were not good jabs, and I think they elevated Nakaya Nielson's confidence because he threw a powerful kick. Before the kick had a chance to land, however, I dropped low and shot for his legs, dumping him hard to his back.

In a matter of seconds I had isolated one of his arms and slapped on a key lock, which put pressure on his elbow and shoulder. Nakaya Nielson had two reactions—he began screaming in pain and furiously slapping his gloved hand against my back. He was trying to tap in submission, let the referee know that he was done fighting, but there was some confusion. Nakaya Nielson had wanted a Muay Thai kickboxing referee to be the other man in the ring with us so the fight would lean in his favor. But there was a downside to that, as Nakaya Nielson was now learning. The referee had no idea what a submission hold was. He thought Nakaya Nielson was trying to punch me in the back. He thought Nakaya Nielson was screaming out of anger. Since the referee wasn't stopping the bout, I kept cranking on the hold. I could hear the tendons and gristle in Nakaya Nielson's arm and shoulder crackling, and still I cranked on the hold. Nakaya Nielson was screaming really loud by this point, "AAAaaaaaaa," and the referee was looking at him like, *What? What does he have? What is he doing to you?*

It took at least ten seconds for the referee to realize that his boy was in some serious pain and pull me off him. With Nakaya Nielson rolling around on the ground, cupping his mangled arm, I stood up and the crowd went nuts. Forty thousand people went absolutely nuts. There hadn't been any highflying stunts or flashy strikes; yet they loved it. Right then I knew that mixed martial arts competition was going to be the sport of the future.

After that exciting bout, it was difficult to go back to pulling my punches and releasing my submission holds while in the ring. I loved professional wrestling, don't get me wrong, but I loved reality combat even more. I had no idea what was going on over in Brazil, that they had been holding mixed

martial arts tournaments for half a century. I thought we were breaking new ground by having fighters from different martial arts disciplines square off against each other, and I loved every minute of it. I loved it because in a real fight I was master of my own destiny.

Professional wrestling wasn't so bad when the fans knew the bout was worked, but that wasn't always the case. I remember one time Fujiwara wanted me to put him over in a worked shoot. Everyone would think the match was real, only I would lose. I had to pull my punches, and I couldn't kick. I understood that's the way the business worked, but I didn't want to do that anymore. I didn't want people thinking that I was getting my butt kicked when in fact I wasn't. I gritted my teeth and bore it, but when Suzuki and Funaki came to me in secret and said that they were thinking of starting their own organization, one that was going to be more shoot and less work, I was all ears.

I was the biggest foreigner in Japan at the time, and they needed me in order to get their organization off the ground. It was a big risk to take. If I went with them and their organization failed, my professional wrestling career in Japan would most likely be done. Fujiwara wouldn't have taken me back, and the other organizations probably wouldn't have taken me in either. Despite what I had riding on the line, the decision didn't take long to make. In addition to wanting to fight, I was also deeply loyal to Funaki. I wouldn't have gotten where I am today without him. Fujiwara offered me a substantial raise to stay, but I didn't take it. I had made up my mind—I was going to fight for a living.

4

A Glimpse of the Future

WHILE FUNAKI AND SUZUKI WERE GETTING things organized in Japan for the first Pancrase event, I returned home. With no more ties in North Carolina, the family moved back to California and settled in Lodi, a midsized town in the north of the state. It was a great place to raise a family, but it wasn't the best location for what I was trying to do. If I was going to start fighting, real fighting, then I needed to keep up on my training, spar for at least a couple of hours every day. The problem was I had no one to spar with.

In an attempt to solve that problem, I started going around to all the karate schools in Lodi and Sacramento. I was a pretty big kid, and I'd go into a place and approach the head instructor. Almost every time, I had the same conversation.

"What you looking for?" the instructor would ask.

"I'm training for some fights, and I need someone to punch and kick at me. Perhaps do some grappling."

"Oh, that's great," he would say. "Sounds really interesting. I don't think this would be the right place, but I know of a dojo that's probably right down your alley."

He would give me the name and location of this other school, and I would head over there. I'd talk with the instructor, he'd tell me it sounded real interesting, and then he'd send me to another school. None of the instructors wanted to train with me because everyone in their school thought they were the toughest fighters on the planet. If they did some sparring and got their ass handed to them, they would no longer be the toughest fighter on the planet. It would hurt their business, so they locked me out.

It got really frustrating, and I eventually gave up on trying to spar with people who already knew, or thought they knew, how to fight. Instead I searched for people who knew absolutely nothing about fighting so I could build them up from scratch. It was slow going in the beginning, but eventually I stumbled upon Vernon White, my first student. He was a gifted athlete who was eager to learn, so every afternoon we worked out in the attic of my home. Submission fighting is nothing like karate—there are no katas or flashy punches and kicks. There are no belt tests or secret moves. If someone puts in the time and hard work, he can usually excel relatively quickly, and that is what Vernon did. It didn't take long until he could put up enough of a fight to give me the kind of workouts I needed to stay in shape.

Word started to get around, and soon more young men who knew absolutely nothing about fighting started dropping by. It was hard to convince them that what we were doing was going to be the wave of the future because everything was so informal—we were training in my attic, for crying out loud. I had made some decent money over in Japan, so I decided to open up my first school. It wasn't much, just a small storefront in a local strip mall, but I still felt it deserved a name. I didn't want the name to give people the wrong impression—I didn't want them to think it was another karate school. I toiled over it for quite a while, but then one afternoon I was watching a National Geographic special on lions. They talked a lot about the lion's den, the lion's home, and how lions will creep off into the grass to go hunting. It seemed to fit what I was trying to establish. I didn't want a bunch of guys who felt like they had to bow to me or go through ridiculous rituals. I wanted the gym to be a home away from home for everyone who was a part of it. I wanted it to be a gym full of ruthless fighters.

As I was getting my gym off the ground, I got word from Funaki that the first Pancrase event was going to be held on September 21, 1993, in Tokyo Bay Hall. Suzuki was going to be on the card, as well as Bas Rutten, a famous Dutch kickboxer. The organization wanted more Americans on the card to build controversy, and I told him that I'd gotten Vernon up to speed. We decided to pair him against Takaku Fuke, the second young boy I had wrestled when I went through my tryout over in Japan a few years prior. The card was starting to fill up, but Funaki and I still weren't in the mix. I asked him what was going on, and he said that he had arranged it so that he and I would fight in the main event.

I trained hard for that one—had to. Funaki is the best submission wrestler out there.

When it came down to fight night, I wasn't nervous; yet I wasn't calm. Funaki was my instructor, a man I deeply respected. If it weren't for him, I would never have gotten as far as I did. But the moment we climbed into that ring, our friendship would have to be put aside. It wasn't going to be like those thousands of sparring matches we'd had in the gym. We wouldn't pull our punches and kicks, and we wouldn't go easy on the submission holds. When we stepped into that ring, we were going to try and hurt each other.

The under card fights went really well. Suzuki caught his opponent in a rear naked choke in less than four minutes. Rutten, who would later claim the heavyweight title of the UFC, knocked his opponent out in forty-three seconds. Vernon did well, but Fuke caught him in an arm bar in a little over a minute. You could tell by looking out into the audience that the bouts weren't what the crowd was used to. They had grown accustomed to long, drawn out fights full of reversals and close calls. These were real fights, and I think the crowd recognized the difference. I think it confirmed their suspicions that what they had been seeing all those years in professional wrestling was just a little too dramatic to be real.

Then Funaki and I climbed into the ring. Both of us were extremely popular in Japan at the time, and we had the crowd hanging on the edge of their seats. It wasn't a one-sided beating, that's for sure, but I did manage to catch him in a chokehold that forced him to tap in submission in a little over six minutes. It was the first time I had beaten him. It was a big victory for me, but it was also a big victory for Funaki.

He was the one who had trained me, the one who taught me everything I knew.

The first event was a huge hit with the Japanese public, and over the next few months everything skyrocketed. After fighting in two more events, suddenly there were Ken Shamrock video games, Ken Shamrock posters, Ken Shamrock T-shirts. I was in over a dozen magazines each month, and my face was all over the news. Pancrase was becoming the biggest thing in Japan since rice, and for a while I was the star of the show.

The organization was growing so fast that they were in desperate demand for fighters. The Japanese public particularly liked the matches between Japanese and foreign fighters, so part of my job became recruiting Americans to fight over in Japan. The organization basically wanted fresh meat, bodies for their fighters to beat up in the ring. I wasn't about to do that. I wasn't going to go up to someone on the street and say, "Dude, I got this fight, you want to go?" If I did that, I knew what would happen. The guy would get his ass handed to him in the ring, and then he would come back to me and say, "Why did you do that to me?" I didn't want to have that on my conscience. I made it real clear to the organization that if I was going to send fighters over, they were going to be prepared.

In order to do that, I moved the gym out of the strip mall and into a warehouse in an industrial district of Lodi. In one room I had weight-lifting equipment, every machine you could think of. In another room, I had 2,550 square feet of mats. And in the third room, I had a full-sized ring and dozens of punching bags hanging from the ceiling. There were no fancy pictures or weapons hanging on the wall. It was a hard-core training facility. It was perfect.

Once I had the gym set up, I then had to fill it up with young fighters. It was different from trying to get people packed into a karate school. There was no way I could accept just anyone who wanted to learn how to fight. A lot of people think they want to learn how to fight, but when it comes time to actually climb into that ring, they suddenly realize that they can't handle the stress. Then all that hard work and instruction just goes down the drain. I wasn't offering self-defense classes. I wasn't trying to boost anyone's self-esteem. I was in the business of turning out fighters.

In an attempt to find those fighters, I did the same thing the Japanese had done to me when I first went over for the UWF. I held a tryout. I didn't invent or create the tryout; I just stole it from the Japanese and brought it to the United States. It was hard, but no harder than what I had gone through. I broke the young hopefuls down with an hour of extreme physical fitness. Running, sprints, and hundreds of push-ups, sit-ups, and squats. Every so often one of them would make it through this hell, and then I'd toss them into the ring and beat up on them for a solid hour. I caught them in arm bars and chokeholds. I wrenched on their knees and ankles. Seldom did one of the hopefuls make it through the second stage of abuse, but there were a few.

And those chosen few were the ones that I accepted into the Lion's Den. If it was still something that they wished to pursue, I shaved their head and put them up in my fighters' house. I didn't coddle or pamper them. I put them in an extreme amount of pain every day in training. They were young, and they needed to know what they were getting into right from the get-go. I didn't want them to step into the ring and go, "I didn't realize it was going to be this hard." I showed them how hard it was going to be in training. I showed them on a regular basis. I paid for their room and board, but I took total control of their lives. I told them when they could eat, when they had to work out, and when they could go out and have fun. I wasn't trying to be a dictator; I was trying to get them ready for the hardest thing they would probably ever have to do—climb into a ring with a Japanese submission master and engage in full-out hand-to-hand combat. When they stepped into that ring, I wanted their fight to be easy compared to what they had gone through in training.

There were many broken bones along the way, but it paid off. If you have followed the careers of the Lion's Den's fighters, then you know that nearly all of my guys won their first fight. Jerry Bohlander, Mikey Burnett, Pete Williams, Guy Mezger, and my adopted brother Frank, they all won their first fight. And most of those fights were championship bouts.

My guys got so proficient in submission fighting that the Japanese fighters started coming to the States to train with us. They lived in the fighters' house with all the young boys and got a different perspective. One thing they adopted was the Lion's Den diet. If you watch the first Pancrase fight, most of the Japanese fighters were chubby. They were in excellent shape, capable of fighting for long periods of time without getting winded, but they had an extra row of flab around their middle. While they were in

my fighters' house, I put them on an extensive weight-lifting program, and instead of feeding them cabbage, potatoes, and soup, I fed them steak, chicken, and rice. In a matter of months, you could see a noticeable difference. The Japanese fighters stepping into the ring were all buffed out and ripped to the bone. When the Japanese public wanted to know their secret, Pancrase put out a training video of my diet and played it off as its own.

I didn't mind; things were going too well to worry about small matters. I had a great group of fighters back home, I was one of the most popular fighters over in Japan, and I had a wonderful family. I believed I had found my path, the road I was going to travel for some time, and then one day I came across an ad in *Black Belt* magazine for the first Ultimate Fighting Championship. Promoters were looking for experienced martial artists to compete in a bare-knuckle tournament that had no rules or weight classes. It caught my attention, but I was also skeptical. For several years I had wanted to get involved in fighting in the States, but every time I heard about a "no rules" event, it always petered out. And when it didn't peter out, it was fixed or rigged. My father convinced me to answer the ad, so I did. Then I put it out of my mind. At the time I had no idea how big it was going to be, or that the Ultimate Fighting Championship would consume the next several years of my life.

5

Sweat, Blood, and Sacrifice

I CONTACTED PANCRASE THE MOMENT I GOT accepted into the first UFC. Pancrase was always a little skeptical about their fighters competing in other organizations because if their fighters lost, it made Pancrase look bad. I told them who was putting the event on, a Brazilian family by the name of Gracie, so they did some research and rustled up some tapes on Royce Gracie. We all sat down and watched them, and none of us were impressed. It was obvious that he knew how to grapple, but he didn't look all that good. Since he was the favorite to win the event, I took the tournament pretty lightly.

Still doubtful that the event would actually take place, I followed through with my commitment to fight in Pancrase just three days prior to the first UFC. Then, still banged up from the fight, I hopped on a flight to Denver. The moment I got off the plane, I realized I had forgotten one small detail—Denver was a mile high, and I hadn't left enough time to get acclimated to the elevation. Just as I started to get worried, I saw the other combatants. The majority of them were karate practitioners and kickboxers. If they were just as disillusioned as Don Nakaya Nielson about what made a good fighter, then I figured I wouldn't have to worry about losing my breath.

There were a couple of days of interviews and talking with the press, and then we all converged backstage at the McNichols Arena on the night of November 12, 1993. Royce Gracie had a separate dressing room, and the rest of us were all packed into one warm-up room. I remember Kevin Rosier was scheduled to fight Zane Frazier in the second bout of the evening, and he was doing a little interview a couple of feet away from me. When asked how he planned to beat Frazier, he said something like, "Well, I'm going to let him punch out. I'm going to let him hit me, get tired, and then I'm going to knock him out." The moment I heard that, I thought, *You're crazy. This is bare knuckles, man. This isn't like a boxing match. You can't cover up and let your opponent get tired hitting you.*

So an hour or so later, I'm warming up for my first fight, and Kevin Rosier and Frazier head down to their Octagon, the eight-sided fighting pit of the UFC. I still couldn't get what Rosier had said out of the back of my mind, so I decided to go see who came out on top. As it turned out, Rosier followed his game plan to a tee. He went out there and let Frazier beat on him with everything he had. Rosier was bleeding all over the place, getting the living hell kicked out of him, and then all of a sudden Frazier got tired. That's when Rosier opened up with punches, knocked Frazier to the ground, and then stomped on his head. Fight over. In the postfight interview they asked Rosier how he did it, and he said, "I let him punch out." I was thinking, *There's something wrong with this guy*. Right then and there I knew that this was the real deal.

Twenty minutes later it was my turn in the Octagon. My opponent was Patrick Smith, a kick-boxer who'd won some pretty tough full-contact karate tournaments by blasting his opponents with barrages of punches and kicks. He was a confident kid, certain he was going to knock Ken Shamrock on his ass. In his prefight interview, he'd boasted that he was impervious to pain. I thought I'd put that statement to the test, so immediately after he threw his first kick of the fight, I shot in for his legs. Once I brought him to the ground, I isolated his right leg and dropped back for a heel hook. Before I could really get it sunk, Smith was crying out in pain and tapping his hand in submission.

I had been confident in my skills going into the UFC, but defeating Smith so quickly made me even more confident. I figured I had the tournament in the bag.

My next bout was against Royce Gracie, the competitor everyone had made such a fuss over—the competitor that the whole tournament had been designed around. Throughout the whole show, the commentators were talking about Brazilian jujitsu this, Brazilian jujitsu that. Well, I planned to stomp a mud hole in Brazilian jujitsu. And things went as planned in the beginning of our match. I shot in for Royce's legs, took him to the ground, and obtained the top position. I had just defeated Smith with a heel hook, so I thought I might try the same thing on

Royce. When I dropped back, however, I didn't realize that Royce had wrapped a part of his uniform around my arm. So as I lay back, it basically pulled him up on top of me. Then I couldn't get my arm out of his uniform to apply the heel hook. To get the leverage I needed, I turned on my side. Royce had one of his hands on my throat, but I wasn't all that concerned because you generally need two hands or two arms to apply a chokehold, and Royce's hand that wasn't on my throat was tied up with my arm. So I was working to apply the heel hook, thinking I was safe, and then all of a sudden I start feeling Royce's *gi* (uniform) tighten around my throat. It got tighter and tighter, and then I couldn't breathe. I had two choices—tap or pass out. I tapped.

I handled the defeat with class, but it got to me. Royce hadn't beaten me because he was a better grappler—he had beaten me because I had never before fought someone wearing a uniform. I didn't understand how it could be used against me. The more I thought about it, the angrier I got. I wanted revenge. I promised that I would get revenge.

So began the feud with Royce Gracie.

The day I got back to the Lion's Den, I dressed up all my training partners in uniforms and proceeded to learn everything about the gi. I learned how it could be used against me, and how I could use it against the person wearing it. I didn't know if the UFC had been a success, if they would ever hold another event, but I trained like they were. I felt as though Royce had stolen something from me, and I was determined to get it back.

You could imagine how excited I was when I learned that they were going to have UFC 2, which was to be held on March 11, 1994. I trained hard for the fight—probably too hard. While sparring with

Vernon White, I broke my hand trying to block a kick to the head. I didn't think it was that big of a deal, but when I went to the hospital, the doctors told me otherwise. They said that if I didn't take time off and let my hand heal, I might never fight again. I didn't have much choice; my revenge would have to wait a little while longer. That only made my anger grow.

Six months later at UFC 3, I was determined not to let anything get in my way. Royce had won the first two tournaments by submitting every competitor who stepped into the Octagon with him. Everyone was talking about Brazilian jujitsu, including Royce. He bragged how he was the best fighter, how nothing could stand the test against Brazilian jujitsu. I knew that that was wrong, and I wanted to show the whole world it was wrong. I wanted to fight him in the first bout of the night, prayed that we would fight in the first bout of the night, but that's not how things played out. Gracie and I were on opposite sides of the quarter bracket. If we were going to square off, both of us would have to defeat our first two opponents.

My first bout of the evening was against Christophe Leninger, a judo player who'd been on the U.S. Team. Judo players are tough, and they are generally pretty talented on the ground, but that doesn't mean that they can take a punch. I figured that once I whacked Leninger around a little bit, his game would go right out the window, which is exactly what happened. When he shot in, I dropped an elbow to his neck, stunning him a little. Then, once we were on the ground, I batted him around until he curled up into a ball. Once I got him doing that, it was pretty much over. I beat on his face and body until he tapped in submission.

My next bout was against Felix Lee Mitchell, an accomplished striker who turned out to be as tough as nails. He put up one hell of a fight, but eventually I took his back and caught him in a rear naked choke.

On the opposite side of the quarter bracket, Royce was having a rough time. His first opponent of the night was Kimo Leopoldo, a powerful street brawler. Royce won the bout, but not before taking a substantial amount of abuse.

While Royce was gearing up for his second fight, I got prepared to meet him in the finals. I was excited about the fight, as were the fans. They knew I had been hunting for his head since our first encounter, and now it was finally going to happen. I was going to prove to everyone that our first encounter had been a fluke and that Brazilian jujitsu was in no way, shape, or form superior to submission fighting. Before I got a chance to do that, however, I received some bad news backstage. The moment Royce had stepped into the Octagon for his second fight of the night, his corner threw in the towel. Apparently his bout with Kimo had taken its toll.

I was crushed. My reason for entering the tournament was to fight Royce, and now that fighting Royce was no longer an option, I no longer wanted to fight in the tournament. When the promoters came backstage to see if I was ready for the final match, I told them I wasn't going to fight. I didn't care about the prize money. All I cared about was Royce. That's how obsessed I was.

I thought the fourth UFC was going to be our winning number, but it wasn't. I had been competing in Pancrase during all of this, and they had me scheduled to compete in one of their events on the exact same day as UFC 4, which was held on

December 16, 1994. If it would have been an ordinary Pancrase tournament, I would have protested, but it was not your ordinary tournament. Over the last couple of years Pancrase had produced many, many champions, and now they were holding one tournament to declare the ultimate champion—The King of Pancrase. No matter how much I wanted to fight Royce, this was more important. I had a contract with Pancrase; it was where I had gotten my start in the fight world. I didn't have a choice.

Backstage at Ryogoku Sumo Hall on the first night of the King of Pancrase Tournament, you could tell it was going to be dog-eat-dog. All the top competitors were there—Minoru Suzuki, Manabu Yamada, Matt Hume, Bas Rutten, Alex Cook, Maurice Smith, Takaku Fuke, Masakatsu Funaki, Jason Delucia, Vernon White, and my brother Frank. Yeah, my guys were in the event too, and as skilled as they had become, there was a better than good chance that I would have to face one of them in the finals. I'm telling you, dog-eat-dog.

The preliminary bouts of the evening were nonstop action. Suzuki beat Hume. Frank polished off famous Dutch kickboxer Rutten. Vernon put away Leon Dinky. Smith, the infamous kickboxer from the States, slam-dunked Fuke. Funaki beat Todd Bjornethun, and I tapped out Cook, a jujitsu fighter from Australia.

That would have been a complete night in and of itself, but it wasn't over yet. Things got more interesting in the second round. The competition got tougher. After our names were drawn backstage, I learned that I was to fight Smith. I had never fought him before, but I had certainly seen him in action. He was one of the best fighters in the world when it

came to kickboxing. He was still new to the sport of mixed martial arts, but he was definitely not one to overlook.

I saw Smith backstage while we were waiting for our turn in the ring, and I could tell he was a little bit nervous. He didn't have a real good grasp on the whole grappling thing yet.

"If you get my ankle, don't break it," he said to me jokingly.

"Cool," I said. "If you hit me, don't knock me out."

That's how fighting usually was in Japan—laid back until you got into the ring. And when Smith and I got into the ring, we did what we knew how to do—he tried to punch and kick and I took him down. I ended up catching him in a heel hook in less than five minutes.

I had won my first two matches, which meant that I was now invited to come back the following day and see if I could win two more matches. If I could manage such a feat, then I would be declared the King of Pancrase. The fierce Japanese competitor Manabu Yamada had knocked Frank out of the tournament, and Funaki knocked out Vernon. I was sad that they had lost, but I was also relieved that I didn't have to fight them. I'm not saying that I would have beaten them or they would have beaten me. All I'm saying is that we were family, and in the tournament to declare the King of Pancrase, as I said before, it was dog-eat-dog.

In my first bout the following night, I found myself back in the ring with Funaki, my instructor. We had gotten sort of used to fighting each other at this point, knew each other's movements and setups, so it was quite a back-and-forth battle. In the end, however, I ended up catching him in a submission in less than six minutes. Yamada put away Suzuki in their match, so I ended up stepping into the finals with Yamada. He was a short, stocky Japanese kid, but he was tough. I almost caught him in several submissions, but each time he managed to squirrel his way free. After going for thirty minutes straight, the bout fell into the hands of the judges, and I was given the decision.

What I had accomplished didn't sink in until I heard the roar of the crowd. I was an American competing in a tournament designed for the Japanese, and I won. I beat them all on their home turf. It validated everything I had worked for in the last several years. The sweat, the blood, the sacrifice. In that moment, I truly felt like a king. I couldn't help but get a little teary-eyed.

In addition to a heaping dollop of pride, there were other things to come out of that tournament. After the show, I talked with Maurice Smith. He really wanted to get into the mixed martial arts fighting, but he felt he wouldn't be able to excel like he wanted to until he learned how to grapple. We decided to strike a deal. He would come out to the Lion's Den in California and I would teach him the art of submission. In exchange, he would help my guys and me with our punches and kicks. Both of us followed through on the agreement, and soon all of us in the Lion's Den had a whole slew of new strikes tucked in our arsenal.

And there were a lot of people in the Lion's Den at this point. The UFC had brought submission wrestling to the forefront of the martial arts world. People knew that I lived in Lodi, California, so they started looking me up and asking what it took to join my gym. I always told them the same thing—you have to pass the tryout. Although the tryouts didn't get any easier, more people started to pass because of the sheer numbers. I had people coming from all over the world, and our fighting camp became a force to reckon with.

The only thing that still nagged at me and made my life seem somehow incomplete was the revenge I needed to get on Royce. My father was managing my career, and he was still angry that I had backed out of UFC 3. He knew why I had done it, that I didn't care about the money or the belt, but he felt that I had let down my fans. I supposed I did in a way, but revenge is a funny thing—it blinds you to everything else. As a result, my father said he would no longer support me in a tournament-style format. He talked with the owners of the UFC to see what they could do about setting up a special bout so Royce and I could finally meet. As it turned out, it was on their minds as well. Many of the fans were growing impatient to see the two of us square off. It was about time that we got down to business.

In UFC 5, held April 7, 1995, the first Superfight was born. Knowing this time nothing could stop me from getting to Royce, I started developing a game plan in my mind. His whole bragging system was, *I'm in better condition, my skills are better, and I can beat anybody, anyplace, anywhere, anytime.* I wanted to shut that bragging system down. To do that, I wasn't going to open with a flurry of punches. I was going to go in there, take him down, and then slowly wear him out, make him so dog-ass tired that he couldn't even stand. I was going to beat on his ribs and face, tear him apart piece by piece. And then, when he was lying gassed on the canvas, I was going to treat him like a baby. I was going to show the whole world that his conditioning wasn't better, that his style wasn't better. That he couldn't beat Ken Shamrock anywhere, anyplace, anytime.

In training, I prepared for a two-hour fight. By the time that two-hour mark rolled around in our fight, I would be doing whatever I wanted to him.

Then, two days before our battle was to happen, I got some bad news. The owners of the UFC pulled me into a room and told me that a thirty-minute time limit had been put in place. I kept my cool, but I definitely didn't like what I was hearing. My whole strategy was to take Royce the long haul, beat him up over time. Now that I had only thirty minutes to put him away, it wrecked my whole game plan.

Sometimes you just have to suck it up when things don't go your way, so that's what I did. I climbed into the Octagon with Royce, and I stuck with my original strategy. I took him down, obtained the top position, and then slowly chopped away. If you watch the fight, you will see that everything I did was totally planned out, totally strategic. There were no big moves, just a lot of short, choppy punches. And it worked perfectly. After thirty minutes had expired and still no victor had been declared, the referee stood us up and gave us a couple extra minutes to see if one of us could come out on top. In the very beginning of the fight, I tried to land a punch and missed it. Well, now that I had beat on Royce's ribs and face for the last thirty minutes, he wasn't as quick or agile. I threw the exact same punch I did in the beginning of the fight, only now I landed it, swelling one of his eyes shut.

Time expired before I could chop Royce down for good, but I still considered it a victory. I didn't have a scratch on my face, and Royce was so beat up his brothers had to literally carry him from the ring. I felt all the bad blood had been handled, but I almost found that somewhat sad. Although Royce and I had always had bad intentions for each other,

there was something special about our rivalry. The majority of other competitors in the UFC were just trying to knock each other's heads off. Royce and I were tacticians; we were both primarily grapplers. At the time, grappling was new and mysterious, and people found our conflict inspiring. Once I had beaten Royce up in the ring, it almost seemed like the death of an era to me.

I did, however, have other rivalries in the UFC, such as the one I had going with Dan Severn. Since Royce had backed out of the UFC after my assault, I retained one slot in the next Superfight, and the other slot would be filled with the winner of the regular tournament in UFC 5. That winner happened to be Severn. Everyone called him The Beast, but I had no idea why. He didn't seem beastly in any shape, manner, or form, except maybe how he was always using the same T-shirt to wipe his underarms and face. So after he won the tournament in UFC 5, we were to square off in UFC 6, held on July 14, 1995. The winner of our bout would become the Superfight Champion. Well, a couple days before we were to fight I heard that the odds in the gambling halls were seventy to thirty, and they were in his favor. It was crazy. I had no idea what people were looking at. He was a good wrestler, but that's all that he was. He didn't know how to punch or kick or lock in submission holds. I honestly didn't know how people thought he was going to beat me.

So going into the press conference for the fight I was already agitated. There was Dan, Oleg Taktarov, and me sitting up at the front of the room, and we all had our managers with us. The press started off by asking all of us a few questions, and then they focused on me. I guess Dan thought they were focusing too much on me because he suddenly got up and

Slugging it out with Tito Ortiz in UFC 40.

walked out of the room. I was right in the middle of saying something, and I took it as an insult. I leaned over to Phyllis Lee, who was his manager at the time, and I said, "I was just going to beat him, but now I'm going to hurt him."

"In your dreams," she said in return, and then stormed off.

Well, I guess I was having pretty good dreams that night because I caught Dan in a guillotine choke and forced him to pound his hand in submission a little over two minutes into the fight.

With the bright and shiny Superfight belt wrapped around my waist, I remained on the top of the pile. My next opponent was Oleg Taktarov, a

Russian Sambo master. While I had been fighting Severn at UFC 6, he had been wrecking shop in the regular tournament. Having taken home the tournament belt, he now had the next shot to rid me of the Superfight belt at UFC 7, held September 8, 1995.

I knew Oleg quite well—he trained with us at the Lion's Den. He was a friend of mine. By that point I had become quite accustomed to fighting my friends because in Japan the fighting circle was rather small, and nearly everyone was your friend. But I had to approach the fight with Oleg a little differently. He was as tough as nails, and I knew that if I caught him in a heel hook or an arm bar, he wouldn't tap out. The only way to win the match by submission was to break his arm or leg and have the referee call the bout. I didn't want to do that. In addition to being his friend, I was also trying to get him into Pancrase at the time. If I broke his leg, it would be some time before he could compete again, and he needed the money. So I figured my best chance of winning the fight without seriously injuring him was to beat on him with punches. The chances of knocking him out were slim because of his hard head, but he was a bleeder. If I could open a cut and get him to start pouring blood, I could get a referee stoppage.

It wasn't the best game plan going into a fight, but considering the circumstances it seemed like the best option available. And it turned out just fine. I battered him around for the duration of the match, the bout was declared a draw, and when Oleg recovered, he went on to fight in Pancrase.

I followed that bout up with a more decisive victory in UFC 8, held on February 16, 1996. I took on Kimo Leopoldo, the powerful street brawler who had given Royce Gracie a run for his money in UFC 3. He was a tough and powerful kid, and he even managed to put me on my back, which is rare. Well, he didn't exactly put me on my back. I went for a submission hold and lost my dominant position, but I ended up on my back nonetheless. Not many people had seen me on my back, and everyone thought that Kimo would do the same kind of damage to me as he had done to Royce Gracie. I didn't fear such a thing for several reasons. First, Kimo had clung on to Royce's uniform to help get leverage for his strikes, and submission grapplers like myself don't wear a uniform. Second, I had no intention of lying around on my back and letting Kimo beat on me.

Submission fighters aren't like Brazilian jujitsu practitioners in that they don't lie on their back and wait for an opening. They know how to scramble, and that's exactly what I did.

It just so happens that I scrambled right into a submission. With Kimo standing above me, looking to throw some hard downward strikes, I rolled underneath him and sunk in a knee bar. To get the street brawler to tap in submission, all I had to do was apply pressure.

Things were going great for me on paper, but I started to get a little burnt out. Fighting in the UFC, fighting in Pancrase, and training countless fighters for their fights was all starting to take its toll. Taking a break wasn't an option, so I forced thoughts of fatigue out of my mind and pushed myself harder than ever for my next Superfight bout, which was a rematch with Dan Severn.

I knew catching him wouldn't be so easy this time. He had worked on his striking and had even thrown a few submissions into his sack of tricks. He wasn't going to catch me in a submission, that's for damn sure, but he was improving his game. So, just as I had with Gracie, I trained for a two-hour war. Every day in practice I did two-hour round robins. I got Tra Telligman, Guy Mezger, Vernon White, and several other guys to stand around the ring. They would come at me one at a time, each for ten minutes straight, and we would beat the hell out of each other. After one guy's time was up, the next one would come at me. I did this for two hours straight, no breaks. By the end of my training, I was ready for war. But, just as in the Gracie bout, they changed the rules at the last minute. The fight was taking place in Detroit, Michigan, and the UFC lawyers had been in court for the past couple of days. The UFC had grown real popular by that point, attracting attention both good and bad. There were those who wanted to shut the event down, and it appeared they were having some luck in Michigan courts. The UFC managed to pull out a victory, but not without some sacrifices. The show could go on, but the competitors could not punch. To ensure that no one punched, the district attorney and a couple of cops would be sitting in the audience. If anyone punched, they would be arrested after the show. They told me this just a couple of hours before the fight.

Promoters told me not to worry about it. They told me to go ahead and punch, and they would pay any fines that resulted. It wasn't that easy for me. I was a codirector at a group home, and for the past couple of years I had been lecturing at Juvenile halls, telling kids that they could be whatever they wanted to be so long as they didn't break the law. What kind of statement would I be making if I willingly broke the law on worldwide pay-per-view? I told my dad that I wasn't going to punch, and he thought I was crazy. He said I had to think of the fans out there, many of whom had traveled a long way to see me fight. But to me it just wasn't worth it. Backing out wasn't an option, not with the promoters having spent all that money advertising the main event, so I would just have to go out there and find a way to win without punching.

The problem was I didn't look for a way to win. I went into the fight with a meniscus tear, a cracked rib, and a broken nose. Back in the old days, none of that would have mattered. The moment I stepped

into the ring, I wouldn't have cared about my physical well-being. That didn't happen in the Severn fight. Instead of engaging, taking the fight to him, I stood in the center of the ring while he circled around me. I stood there because I was trying not to get even more injured than I already was. I've said it time and again—that was the most boring fight in UFC history, nothing more than a thirty-minute dance. People started throwing food into the Octagon, and I didn't blame them. I hadn't gone in there with bad intentions.

Dan won that fight by decision, but I don't think he should have. Neither one of us should have won. I remember not long after the bout I was on a plane with Art Davies, the UFC matchmaker, coming back from an event. I had a few drinks under my belt, and I turned to him and said, "You know that fight I had with Severn, the second one. I thought I won that fight."

"No, the judges were right," Davies said.

"How did I lose that fight?"

"Well," he said, thinking about it. "He landed more punches."

"Yeah, but correct me if I'm wrong—weren't punches illegal in that fight?"

I was poking fun, but deep down something was bothering me. I had been fighting nonstop in both the UFC and Pancrase for several years. And when I wasn't training for one of my fights, I was training my fighters for their fights. I was starting to get burnt out, and that scared the hell out of me. I mean, come on, I had lost to Dan Severn.

6

The Toll of Battle

THE ULTIMATE ULTIMATE, HELD AT THE STATE FAIR
Arena in Birmingham, Alabama, on December 7, 1996, was a big tournament, perhaps the biggest tournament the UFC had held up to that point. The ongoing battle between Royce Gracie and myself had stolen a lot of the spotlight in the early years, but now there were a bunch of new competitors sowing terror in the Octagon. Fans of the sport wanted to know who was the toughest of them all, so UFC promoters decided to host a tournament of champions. The majority of the top dogs were there, including Don Frye, Tank Abbott, Kimo Leopoldo, and Gary Goodridge. They were all suited up and ready to throw heavy leather.

For the past couple of years I had been the Superfight champion, so instead of entering tournaments I took on the winner of tournaments. But I had something to prove after losing to Dan Severn. There was a lot of talk going around about how some of the guys coming into the sport were better conditioned, more explosive. It was true that the majority of competitors had started cross-training in both striking and grappling, doing what they needed to do in order to be successful in mixed martial arts competition, but their action-packed bouts also had a lot to do with changes in the rules. In the beginning

there were no time limits, so you took your opponent to the ground, obtained a good position, and then held it. You slowly chopped your opponent down over time. The new rules, however, had put a twelve-minute time limit in place. It was a whole lot easier to come out with both guns blazing when you knew a rest period lay just twelve minutes down the road.

If the fans wanted to see explosions, that's what I would give them. I would let everyone know why I had carried the nickname "One Punch Shamrock" for so many years. In preparation for the fight, I took a bunch of my boys to Cincinnati to work out with Kevin Woods, the strength and conditioning coach of the Cincinnati Bengals. When I wasn't kickboxing or grappling, I was doing this crazy program Woods liked to call Dinosaur Training. He had me lifting sandbags and kegs of beer, building the kind of strength that you can't get hefting balanced weight in the gym. And it paid off. In just a few short months, I was a monster. The moment I climbed into the Octagon, I was going to tear my opponent's head off.

That opponent happened to be Brian Johnston, a six-foot-four, two-hundred-forty-pound kickboxer who was also quite proficient on the wrestling mats.

After referee John McCarthy uttered his famous words, "Let's get it on!" Johnston and I circled each other for a moment, and then he threw a kick. That's when I shot for his legs, lifted him off his feet, and dumped him to his back. I trapped him up against the fence and started unleashing with punches. I could have worked to isolate one of his arms or legs and gone for a submission hold, but that wasn't in my game plan. I had come to the Ultimate Ultimate to explode, so that's what I did. I beat on his ribs and face with over two-dozen hard punches.

"Hang in there!" I heard his corner men shout. "Don't give up! If you give up, you're done!"

I could tell Johnston was going through an inner debate. Should he listen to his corner men or should he listen to reason and tap his hand in submission? He wasn't rushing to a decision, so I decided to help him along by continuing to drop bombs. I pounded my right hand into his ribs and face, over and over. I could feel the reverberations of the impacts all the way up my arm, but the guy refused to give in. The kid was tough, hanging on for dear life. But in order to win the tournament and knock all the new warriors in the UFC down a notch or two, I still had two more fights to go. I was burning unnecessary steam, and I started to get frustrated.

I needed this fight to be over and done with. Thanks to the Dinosaur Training, I had some extra power stored in my arsenal, and I unleashed it in a huge right hand. It was a knockout punch, aimed at Johnston's face, but it veered a little off target, as knockout punches often do. The moment my right hand crashed into the top of Johnston's head I felt one of my knuckles cave in. Pain shot up my arm, but I wasn't worried about that. I had been in so

many barroom brawls and back alley scraps over the course of my life that pain almost felt natural. What caused my alarm was that damn knuckle. It was the same knuckle I had broken while training for UFC 2. That injury had almost put me out of the fight game for good, and this felt like the same injury—the exact same injury. If I couldn't fight, then I couldn't take care of my family or the house of fighters I supported. Everything I had worked so hard to achieve would swirl down the drain.

Realizing the middle of a fight was not the time to worry about the future, I got back to the issue at hand. My right hand had gone completely numb, which meant that I couldn't punch with it or use it to lock in a submission hold. There are very few submission holds that you can lock in with only one good hand.

I had softened Johnston up pretty good by that point, and I hoped he was on his way to tapping. I nailed him with some lefts. He cursed under his breath, but he still hung in there. After banging away a little more with my good hand, I realized this wasn't working. That's when I threw my left forearm across Johnston's throat and dumped my weight behind it. It was a rudimentary choke at best, but it did the trick. After gurgling for a few seconds, Johnston tapped his hand in submission.

I got my hand raised, did a quick post-fight interview, and then hurried off to triage backstage to get a damage assessment. The doc told me nothing that I didn't already know; my hand was busted up pretty good. It was too early to tell how badly it had been busted up, but I was most definitely out of the tournament. I was supposed to fight Abbott in the next round, and anyone who followed either of our careers understood that we didn't much care for each other. As a matter of fact, we straight-up didn't like each other. This tournament was our chance to settle our differences, get all that bad blood out of our system. Now that wasn't a possibility, and that put me in a rather foul mood.

So I left triage not only upset about losing my chance to take home the Ultimate Ultimate tournament belt, but also wondering what I would do in the future if my hand was too mangled to fight. All the rage I had conjured up to compete in this tournament was still trapped in my chest, demanding some sort of release. I planned to go back to my hotel, take a hot shower and get some rest. Allow myself some time to cool off. The last person I needed to see at that point was Tank Abbott, but that's exactly who I did see backstage. And, as usual, he had something to say.

If Tank's comment had been about me, perhaps I could have blown it off. But it was about one of my fighters, Jerry Bohlander. That's one of the things about my personality, about how my brain works. If you want to get on my bad side in a heartbeat, say something bad about one of my friends or family members. It flips a switch in my head, shuts down all reason. It makes it impossible to turn the other cheek.

And what Tank said was complete garbage, something he had pulled out of his imaginary world. I understood that his MO was the bad boy of the UFC, that he had built his reputation off his mouth rather than his fighting record, but there is a time and a place for everything, and this certainly wasn't the time or place. Not with my hand busted up, not with my career possibly down the drain.

Tank had called my fighter a "chicken." In recent years, occasionally one of my guys didn't have the conditioning he should have when he stepped in to fight, but not a single one of my fighters has ever lacked heart. Never, not once, has one of my boys been chicken. After going through one of the hardest tryouts known to man, after years of getting beat up by the toughest hand-to-hand fighters on the planet in training, they had all left fear far behind.

Tank was just bitter. In UFC 11, just two months before the Ultimate Ultimate '96, Tank and Jerry had both fought on the card. In Jerry's opening bout, he had gone up against Fabio Gurgel, one of the toughest Brazilian jujitsu fighters out there at the time. It had just been a wicked battle, both fighters laying everything on the line for fifteen minutes straight. The fight had been placed into the hands of the judges, and Jerry had been awarded the decision. He hadn't given up. He had done what he needed to do to win the fight. But he was in bad shape when we got him backstage. He had gotten cut over his eye, he had no gas left, and his mind wasn't all there. His next fight was against Tank, who outweighed him by nearly sixty pounds. Jerry wanted to fight him; he never once said he didn't want to head back out there, but I pulled the plug. Even though I don't like Tank, I'll admit that he hits hard. I didn't want Jerry to take one of those power bombs because he was too fatigued to bring Tank to the ground and work his magic. Jerry was twenty-one years old. He had a bright future in the UFC. So I made a judgment call and told him to sit this one out.

Instead of fighting Jerry, Tank went on to fight Scott Ferrozzo and got beat. Well, Jerry had fought Ferrozzo in UFC 8, held on February 2, 1996, and beat him. That led me to believe that Jerry would probably have had a better than good chance at beating Tank, and I think Tank realized that too. That's probably why the Pit Bull was so riled up. So what does he do? He starts talking trash backstage at the Ultimate Ultimate '96 when I'm in no condition to fight.

I came unglued. When I went for Tank, his gang of thugs blocked my path.

"Come on, Shamrock," one of his boys said. "We're just fooling around."

"You know what, he needs to shut his mouth," I said, pointing at Tank.

"Come on, it ain't nothing. We're just messing with you."

"It is something," I shouted at Tank. "Here is this kid who fought his heart out, and you only have bad things to say about him. I think you better focus on your fight at hand otherwise you'll never make it to the ring."

I waited for Tank to say something back. Tank always says something back. He probably sits around his living room jotting down little comebacks onto a piece of paper and then commits them to memory so he can look cool in public and on television. But this time he didn't say anything back, not a damn word. He just turned and walked away.

That was great, just great. He got me all riled up and ready to fight and then turns and walks away. Now I had all this pent-up rage and nowhere to put it. I went crazy backstage, demanding to get back on camera. My father thought I was going to make an ass out of myself on live pay-per-view, that I'd come across as a raging lunatic, but even filled with rage I wasn't like Tank. I understood that there was a time and place for everything, and the right time to let my hatred for him be known was when the two of us climbed into the cage together. So when I got back

on camera, I told it how it was. I said I was angry at Tank for some of the things that he said about one of my fighters, and that I wanted to fight him. I later told the promoters of the event that I would even fight him for free.

It wasn't until I got back to my hotel room that I managed to calm down. Breaking my hand and then having Tank talk trash had pushed me over the edge, but I wondered how I had gotten so close to the edge to begin with. A broken hand and some trash talking was normal in the fight game, something you learn to deal with. There was something else that had been bothering me for months, and lying in bed in my hotel room that night, I started to figure it out. I was getting burnt out on fighting, losing my desire to compete. Training for a fight isn't like working a nine-to-five job. You have to push yourself past your limits on a daily basis, work through injuries. And I had been competing in the UFC since the beginning, and when I wasn't getting ready for a fight in the Octagon, I was getting ready for a fight over in Japan. The years and years of combat training was starting to take its toll.

Taking a break wasn't an option, not with all my personal responsibilities. Back before I'd gotten married, I could live out of a one-bedroom apartment and cook everything on a George Foreman Grill. That had all changed with the arrival of my children. I needed to put food on the table and clothes on their backs. I had to start saving for their college educations. I didn't want them growing up poor, and the way I kept that from happening was by fighting. I had just recently purchased a ranch house outside of Lodi, California. I planned on building a training facility on my property, along with a residence where

Throwing a hard right cross at Tito Ortiz in UFC 40.

all my fighters could stay. That was not going to be cheap. In order to do all the things that I wanted, to take care of all the people I needed to take care of, I had to make sure that I stepped into the ring on a regular basis.

That created a lot of stress because I started thinking less about winning the fight and more about not getting hurt. It had happened in the Dan Severn fight. That's a part of the reason why I'd gone off to Cincinnati and trained so hard for the Ultimate Ultimate. It's not that I tried to escape my responsibilities; it's just that I realized that in order to be a successful reality fighter, keep the fans chanting your name and the paychecks coming in, you had step

into that cage with nothing to lose.

Things hadn't worked out as I had planned, and now I was lying in a hotel room with a broken hand, more burnt out than ever. I needed to take some time off to let my hand heal, and I hoped the break would let me get my head straight and come back stronger than ever. The moment I followed through with that, however, things started falling apart.

The first thing to go was my contract with Pancrase. Promoters from the organization had tried calling me a couple of times while I was training for the Ultimate Ultimate '96. I had been up in Cincinnati, working hard with Kevin Woods and the boys, and I didn't have time to think about anything but the fight standing before me. I could have called them back, but that's not the way I work. If I don't have something to say, I'll usually say nothing at all. I've never been one for small talk. Well, Pancrase took it personally, and they ended my contract. They even tried canceling the contract of my brother, Frank. Then they stopped inviting Vernon White over to compete. A part of their excuse for cutting the Lion's Den off their roster was that I wasn't sending over enough fighters. I didn't know what they were talking about. For a time, the top six rankings in Pancrase belonged to fighters from the Lion's Den, the seventh spot was a fighter from another gym, and then the eighth ranking belonged to Lion's Den as well.

We were the most respected fighting team in the world at the time, but respect doesn't pay the bills. I had just taken a huge cut in my income. I still had the money I garnered from the UFC, but my contract with them was up and I needed to sign another deal. When we went to do that, however, Bob Meyrowitz, the owner of the UFC, told me that he was going to have to pay me less. Considerably less. It wasn't that he was trying to hoard all the money for himself; it was just that there was a lot less money to go around. The UFC was more popular than ever. The Ultimate Ultimate '96 had been a resounding success. But there were court fees to think about, as well as the future of the sport. Thanks to a few influential senators, the sport looked more and more like it was going to be taken off pay-per-view.

I owed everything I had to fighting, and more particularly, mixed martial arts competition. As I have already mentioned, it put me in a spot where I could walk through life proud of who I was and what I had accomplished. I loved the arena, stepping into the cage, and the camaraderie of the fighters. Sometimes I'd looked up at the crowd after a grueling battle, and it almost felt as if I were a gladiator living in ancient Rome. The thought of leaving that behind sickened and terrified me. But if I stayed with the sport as I wanted, and the crowds and prize money shrank at every event, then my family would suffer. So after much debate, I picked up the telephone and contacted Meyrowitz. I asked him one more time to rethink my contract, and he said he couldn't.

"I appreciate the fairness and all the things you have done for me, but I have to move on," I said. "I cannot make a living doing this unless I get what I am supposed to get."

"I understand," he said sincerely. "And I truly wish you the best of luck."

When I hung up the phone, I got a strange feeling that I had just done something wrong. Fighting had always been there for me, in the good times and in the bad, and now I was walking away from it. I knew it wouldn't be forever, that I would return after my body healed up and I had some money in my pocket, but it still felt strange. I already missed the surge of adrenaline and the roar of the crowd.

7

Under the Lights

WHEN I TOOK A BREAK FROM FIGHTING IN 1996,
I needed to find a job. There weren't a lot of
employers in the real world looking to hire a man
who'd spent a good portion of his adult life climbing into a cage and hurting people, but making the
transition into the real world was not something
that interested me, anyhow. I had come a long way
since I'd wrestled on the East Coast, and I figured
if I played my cards right, I just might be able to
use my popularity in mixed martial arts competition to land a position in one of the larger professional wrestling organizations. To see if I was correct, I contacted Barry Bloom, a big-time manager
in the pro wrestling world, and he put me in touch
with World Championship Wrestling (WCW), the
World Wrestling Federation (WWF), and a couple
of professional wrestling organizations over in
Japan. As it turned out, all of them were eager to
bring me aboard. Vince McMahon, the owner of
the WWF, seemed the most interested out of all of
them. His organization had taken a little dive in the
ratings because some of its matches had become so
overblown with dramatics and gimmicks that many
pro wrestling fans had begun following the WCW
instead. In an attempt to bring those fans back,
Vince wanted to hire a wrestler who could bring

credibility and realism into his
organization. With my fighting background, he
thought I was the perfect guy for the job.

He flew me out so we could meet in person. We
sat down and chatted for a while, and I liked what he
had to say. I had been a little concerned about how
he might want to market me, but Vince thought I
was most marketable just being myself. I would be
the guy who fought in the street, in back alleys, in
barrooms, and in the rings and cages of mixed martial arts competition. I would be the guy who feared
no one. Of course, he would throw a costume on my
back and slap down some theme music to spice
things up a little, but I would be presented to the
fans as Ken Shamrock the man, not some face-
painted abomination. In Vince's own words, I was
going to be a real-life action hero.

I liked his ideas. And once Vince realized that
I liked his ideas, he slid a contract that was probably twenty-six pages in length across the table. He
wanted me to sign on the dotted line right then
and there so I could make my first appearance that
Monday night on *Raw*. I never imagined that things
would move along so quickly, so I hadn't brought
along an attorney. I trusted Vince, but I also knew
that he was a businessman, and a shrewd one at

that. He wasn't going to give me a good deal just because he liked me. He was going to do what was best for him and his company. So instead of signing the contract, I climbed onto a plane and flew home.

I was a little worried that I had made a grave mistake by bailing, but Vince called the next day and asked what it would take to get the deal done. I told him that I needed to have Barry Bloom look over the contract; that was it. A couple of days later, all the contractual issues had been settled. I scratched my name onto the last sheet, and I then became a proud member of the WWF.

I was going to be making a nice sum of money, and I had the potential to make a whole lot more money down the road. But first I had to do well, prove myself. Vince had taken a lot of chances on different kinds of athletes over the years, and not all of them had triumphed. He had brought in well-known football players, basketball players, and body-builders. Many of them had gotten the heave-ho because either they couldn't keep up in the ring or the fans simply thought they were boring. I knew I wouldn't have too much trouble with the keeping up part, but entertaining the fans was a different matter entirely. In mixed martial arts competition I put the fans on the edge of their seats by destroying my opponents in the cage. That's how I made a name for myself. But it didn't work the same way in professional wrestling. Vince could have written a script that had me destroy everyone—The Rock, Stone Cold Steve Austin, The Undertaker—and yet the fans might still have thought I was boring. Professional wrestling wasn't about being a good fighter; it was about being a good entertainer. It was more about the bark than the bite.

I realized that on February 24, 1997. It was just a few days after I'd signed my contract, and Vince thought it would be a good idea to have me ringside for *Monday Night Raw*. I had been told that I was going to be involved in something, but I didn't know what that something was. So I was sitting there, enjoying the show, and Faarooq started tearing into me over the microphone. In addition to calling me a bunch of nasty names, he also started mocking me— "Ooooo, Mr. Tough Guy. Big bad fighter man. You don't look so tough to me."

It had been a long time since I'd been involved in professional wrestling in the United States. I hadn't forgotten about the trash talking, but I had forgotten just how real the person doing the trash talking could come across. And let me tell you, this guy was convincing. At first I was upset, but then I started to get mad. Pretty soon I was irate. I got so irate that I came very, very close to jumping over the rail and throwing blows—real blows.

After the show I was still upset. I saw Faarooq backstage, but when he walked past me, he gave me a friendly nod. That's when I realized that I had almost made a terrible mistake. Faarooq didn't think he could kick my butt. He had been acting. That's right, *acting*. I had forgotten all about that. And if I planned to also be an actor, which was mandatory for the job, then I couldn't go around kicking everyone's head in the moment they started talking a little trash. I had to be able to talk trash right back. As much as I hated to admit it, I needed a trash talking coach. I needed a coach period. I had spent so much time competing in MMA competition that professional wrestling had become foreign to me.

Luckily, Bret Hart came to my rescue. He invited me up to Calgary to train with him and shake loose some of the cobwebs. In addition to knocking the rust off my game, I also walked away with a bunch of professional wrestling tips that proved invaluable. The biggest tip Bret shared with me had to do with selling my holds. I had been under the assumption that using real submission holds was the best way to please the fans. Bret taught me that that wasn't always the case. A lot of fans didn't know which submission holds actually caused pain and which ones were strictly for show, and many of them didn't care. They judged the effectiveness of a hold by reading the body language and facial expressions of the wrestlers in the ring. The fans wanted to know how a wrestler was feeling when he locked in a hold—was he tired, was he cocky, was he mad? They wanted to be able to relate to the two men under the lights.

If I was going to give them what they wanted, I had to overdramatize every movement. Instead of tucking my chin to my chest when locking in a submission hold, which is what you want to do in a real fight, I needed to keep my chin up so that everyone could see my face. Bret taught me a number of these little things, and by the time I walked away from our training session in Calgary, I felt like I had just graduated from Acting 101.

As I worked on making my submissions more dramatic, Vince was getting ready to thrust me into the mix. Instead of kicking off my career with a regular old professional wrestling match, he decided that I should do something special. After talking it over, we thought it was a good idea to do a real fight with one of my Lion's Den fighters, and I brought in Vernon White. We had been training together so long we each knew how the other moved, and I was certain we could put on a good show. We weren't going to try and knock each other out, but we would spar hard enough that the fans would go, "Wait a minute, what the hell are they doing in there? I think they're fighting. Who is this guy?" Then they would do a little research, discover that I had been fighting in a steel cage for the past few years, and then start paying more attention to my matches.

It didn't work out quite as planned, even though Vernon and I beat each other from one side of the ring to the other. I accidentally caught him with a couple of hard blows, first an elbow and then a punch. The punch actually split is face open. He was dripping blood, but all the fans thought it was fake blood, so they were thinking, "Yeah, whatever." Truth be told, I think the majority of fans actually thought our bout was somewhat boring. In wrestling you have people flying off the top ropes, these big dramatic slams to the canvas. In our match we rolled around on the ground, locking in submissions that were hard to see. The fans had come to be entertained, not to see a real fight. That was an important lesson to learn.

I was still trying to work out the kinks in my wrestling when I had my first match with Vader. I knew that Vader had done some matches over in Japan, which meant that he was probably pretty tough. I figured he wouldn't take it personally if I was a little stiff with some of my moves. And he probably wouldn't have taken it personally if I was a little stiff, but with it being my first match and all, I was *really* stiff. I remember telling him before our bout that I was going to grab his head and throw some Muay Thai knees to his midsection, and that he should wrap his arms across his chest to block them. Well, he forgot to cross his arms and I ended up landing a knee to his face. I didn't throw the knee hard, but it was hard enough to break his nose. In addition to this, I also landed several kicks to his legs. Once again I didn't think I threw them hard, but the purple bruises on Vader's thighs proved otherwise.

When we came backstage after the bout, I was certain I had blown it. I truly felt I had ruined my first true match in the WWF. When Bret came up to me, I just shook my head and said, "Oh my God, that sucked!"

"What are you talking about? That was great."

"You're kidding me? I felt like it wasn't there."

"No, dude," he said, patting me on the back. "That was your first match, bro. And it's over."

A few minutes later more wrestlers started coming up and congratulating me. I thought they were all pulling my leg, but when I watched the match on video, I realized that I hadn't done that bad. I still needed a lot of work, especially in the timing department. I needed to learn when to go for a submission, when to throw punches and kicks, and when to escape from a hold. I needed to learn how to blend everything together to create drama. The only reason the match had gotten over was because I had followed Vader's lead. He had saved my ass in a big way. It made me realize that I didn't know as much as I thought I did. Instead of pretending that I was some kind of pro and possibly hurting someone, I sucked up my pride and played student for a while.

It was a big complement to my fellow wrestlers because I was basically telling them, "Hey, I don't entirely know what I'm doing here, and you do. So show me the way." But just because I was willing to hand them the lead didn't mean that they were eager to climb into the ring with me. As a matter of fact, it was the complete opposite. After the bout

with Vader, many wrestlers were concerned that I was going to hurt them in the ring. I heard people say, "I don't want to wrestle with that guy, he's a shooter. He's gonna break my arm with that funky stuff that he does. Those crazy arm and leg locks." They didn't understand submission holds because no one had ever done them before, at least not in the States. I didn't want to give them up, refused to give them up, so to fix the problem I started altering my holds. I took the sting out of them. In a couple of months, most of the wrestlers became comfortable with them, and then a couple of months later, many of the wrestlers started adopting some of my techniques. Before I came into the WWF, rarely did you see a wrestler slap on a submission hold. Now you see them in practically every match. I felt that was my little contribution, and I've always been proud of that.

Vader took a couple of weeks off after our bout to nurse his broken nose and wounded leg, but once he returned, the two of us formed an alliance. We did a program together, and after following his lead for a few weeks, I started to get more and more comfortable in the ring. Our matches started to flow really well. I was very appreciative of how he took me under his wing, but to tell you the truth, I was kind of eager for our partnership to break up. It's not that I didn't like him; I thought he was a great guy. The thing that bothered me was his outfit—it stunk to high heaven. He had the smelliest gloves and wrestling singlet that you could imagine. Before I had done my first match with him, I had heard people backstage say "Oh my god, I have to wrestle Vader tonight," like they were all stressed out about something. I hadn't the slightest clue why they were so worried, but it hit me once I climbed into the ring with him. He didn't wash his clothes, ever. At the end of every night, I would have to go down and buy bleach and detergent at a local convience store just to get the funk out of my clothes—that's how bad it was. And I did a program with him for six weeks!

Enduring the funk had been worth it, however. My program with Vader had been my tryout, my proving ground, and I showed Vince McMahon that I had what it took to entertain the fans. In addition to this, I also think Vince realized that I had more to give. Pretty soon he had me working with everybody. I worked with the Boss Man, then I worked with Owen Hart, and then I worked against Owen. I wrestled Shawn Michaels on *Monday Night Raw*. I wrestled Stone Cold Steve Austin twice on *Raw*, and then I wrestled The Undertaker on pay-per-view. I pretty much wrestled everybody, and I was having good matches. Immediately I was making headway, listening to the fans' cheers grow louder and louder every time I walked down the ramp. And the better I became in the ring, the more creative things got.

Vince decided to cash in on the popularity of my mixed martial arts training camp, the Lion's Den. He built a massive cage that was meant to resemble the Octagon. It didn't look exactly the same—the cage slanted outward so you could fall on it and still fight—but it looked pretty close. Then I climbed into that cage with Steve Blackman, a wrestler well versed in the martial arts. When the match was announced, Blackman dramatically stated that he would fight in my cage so long as there were weapons. So they hung weapons at the top of each corner. There were nunchucks, kendo sticks, all sorts of fun stuff. It was the first time anything like that had ever been done, and it went over really well. In fact, it went over so well that Vince had me

do a bunch of other first-of-their-kind matches. I did a match where I was tied up in a straightjacket, and then I did a match with Blackman in a parking lot surrounded by a ring of cars.

I had a lot of really cool showdowns in the WWF, but perhaps the coolest showdown of all happened outside of the ring. Shortly after I entered the ranks of the WWF, I was with Billy Gunn and several other wrestlers at the airport, waiting for a flight. I can't remember where we were headed, but that's not an important part of the story. What is important is that I'd been hearing things from some of the other wrestlers, things that made my blood boil. I guess while the Nasty Boys had been in the WWF, they had talked a whole bunch of trash about me. They bragged about how they beat me up, put me in the hospital. They bragged about how if they ever saw me again, they were going to tap dance on my face a second time. That was hard to live with.

It seemed at nearly every show one of the wrestlers would come up to me and say, "Hey, Shamrock, how's it going. I saw Knobs not too long ago, and he said you guys got into a fight. He said he kicked your ass."

I had never forgotten about what had happened. I had never lost my desire for revenge, but while competing in the UFC there had been so much going on I had definitely put it on the back burner. But hearing what the Nasty Boys had been saying brought the whole incident back to the forefront of my thoughts. Both of them were gone from the WWF by the time I had gotten in, and that was probably a good thing. I would have killed them in the locker room and lost my job. But I knew that I would run into them sooner or later. And when I did, it wasn't going to be pretty.

So I was standing in the airport with Billy Gunn and a couple of wrestlers, and I saw the Nasty Boys. They were flying off to do some independent show, and they just happened to be in the same airport at the same time. It had been four or five long years, but it was as if I could still feel the welt on my head from where they blindsided me with that metal telephone.

Knobs saw me coming, and he instantly bolted in the other direction. I had never seen anyone run so fast. But the other one, Saggs, the guy who had hit me with the telephone, was already at the counter and didn't see me. I dropped my bag and started walking toward him. I was so mad that my whole body started shaking. I was literally trembling. Never, not in all my hundreds of fights, has that ever happened to me.

Before I could reach him, the guys I was with grabbed me. They didn't care if I beat Saggs up, they just didn't want me to get arrested in the process. I mean, come on, we were in an international airport. "You can get him later, Ken. This isn't the time or place," they kept saying. "You can get him later."

It suddenly registered that I could get them later. If they planned on catching their flight, they would have to go through the terminals. That's where I would confront them. There were generally fewer cops in the terminals, and I'd have more time to do what I needed to do before getting hauled off to jail.

So I headed up to the terminals. There were probably twenty other wrestlers from the WWF all sprawled out on the seats, waiting for the flight. So I took a seat in back of them and kept my eyes trained down the terminal, waiting for one or both of the Nasty Boys to come sauntering up.

Sure enough, a few minutes later, here comes Saggs. He didn't see me sitting there, so he started shooting off at the mouth like he had been for the past five years. He said, "Man, could someone please tell Shamrock to take a chill pill."

Immediately I jumped over the chairs and started throwing him around. With as much trash as he had talked, I expected a fight. I expected that he would square off with me like a man and fight. He had bragged that he would beat me up if he ever saw me again, and now here was his chance. Instead of putting up his hands, however, he dropped his bag and turned his back like a coward.

"If you hit me, it's a federal offense," he shouted. "If you hit me it's a federal offense."

Immediately all of the twenty wrestlers sitting around let loose with a massive, "Ooooo."

"You're pathetic," I said. "You've been saying for so many years how you would beat me up if you saw me, and now you cower like this. You're absolutely pathetic."

I waited for him to say something—I prayed that he would say something. And when he kept his mouth shut and kept on cowering, all the rage and anger drained out of me. All my desire to kill this guy just floated away. Losing face in front of your fellow wrestlers is a big deal, and Saggs had just lost all of his. Since that day, I haven't heard from a single source that either him or his partner have been bragging about how they kicked my ass. I shrunk them both down to size, and if either of them ever feel big enough to step up to the plate, they know where to find me.

8

On the Road

I LEARNED THE TRUE MEANING OF "BEING ON THE
road" in the WWF. I'd travel with a gaggle of
wrestlers from one city to the next for ten days and
then come home for three. Then I'd head back out
for seven days, and then come home for two. When
it was all added up, I was on the road between 180
and 190 days a year. For a while I was on every
weekly show and every pay-per-view. It was great for
my career, don't get me wrong, but my life outside of
wrestling started to suffer.

The first thing to fall apart was the Lion's Den. It
was difficult for many of my fighters to understand
why I had gone to professional wrestling. It was difficult for them to accept that I needed a break from
fighting and was moving on to something else for a
little while. When they heard some of the fighters
from other camps calling me a sellout right after I
left, they got irate, but after hearing the same things
over and over, a part of them started to believe what
they were hearing. My guys were just starting out in
their fighting careers, and they couldn't understand
why I was leaving. They thought I was leaving them,
but that wasn't the case at all. I had to move on in
order to pay for the gym and the fighters' house. I
had many, many mouths to feed, and unless I did
something, the life we had wouldn't last.

So there were some hard feelings
when I left, and those feelings simmered and brewed
and slowly broke down the well-oiled machine
everyone had worked so hard to create. Since I wasn't
around to monitor what the guys ate, when they
trained, and how often they went out, I put my
brother Frank and Jerry Bohlander in charge.
Although I didn't realize it at the time, Frank har-
bored some pretty deep resentment about the decision I had made. He felt I was a traitor, and that
made it difficult for him to put forth the effort
needed to run the gym properly. The fighters weren't
getting the training they needed; the self-defense
classes weren't getting taught. I wasn't quite sure
what was going on, but it certainly wasn't what
should have been.

I was to blame as much as anyone. Being so
hands-on with my fighters worked great when I was
around, but without establishing a clear hierarchy,
the moment the head honcho stepped out of the pic-
ture the Lion's Den was left with fifteen leaders. Each
of those leaders had a different perception of the way
things should be done, and when one decision con-
tradicted another, nothing got done at all. I could
have spent more of my days off down at the gym, but
most of the time I was so burnt out from being on

the road that I'd pass out on the couch at home. And when I wasn't passed out on the couch, I was spending time with my kids.

I had hoped that all the little disputes and problems would work themselves out, but that had been wishful thinking. We had a large group of very different young men forced together for a long period of time. They ate together, trained together, worked together, cruised the town together. There was drama, and in order to keep that drama from getting out of hand, I needed to be around to put my foot down. It was just like MTV's *The Real World* or any of the other reality shows on television. As a matter of fact, the Lion's Den was the original reality show. I'm convinced some producer out there had read my first book, *Inside the Lion's Den*, and then thought, *My god, what a great idea for a television show: It's got drama, it's got late-night brawls, it's got hurt feelings and wonderful moments of sharing and kindness.* If that person would have sent in a camera crew to film the inner workings of the Lion's Den in its height of glory, I guarantee it would have made all the reality shows out there now pale in comparison. But if those same cameramen had tried to film the boys after I went to the WWF, they probably wouldn't have made it out alive. Things got pretty heated there for a little while.

The straw that broke the camel's back was when Frank began negotiating his own contracts to fight. The deal in the Lion's Den was that I paid for all the fighters' food, board, and training, and in return the gym got 15 percent of their purse when they fought. I didn't care about Frank's 15 percent—the money from the guys' fights never came close to paying off their overhead—but it was the principle of the whole thing.

I got the call while I was on the road with the WWF, found out that Frank had gone behind my back, and I was fuming mad. I flew right home and headed straight for the gym. Frank and Jerry were there, as well as a number of other people. I lost my temper and ended up throwing a computer monitor across the room. I was mad at Frank, but I was also mad at how the Lion's Den was falling apart because I wasn't around. I loved every one of my fighters; we were a family. All of us had worked for many, many years to build a gym that was respected around the world, and now it was collapsing. I said and did things I shouldn't have, as did everyone else, but I hoped that it would be a stern wake-up call for all of us. We needed to get back to how things were, reacquire the fire.

Instead of that happening, Frank left the next day. He packed up his stuff, threw it all into the back of the car I had given him, and was gone. That was pretty much the beginning of the end.

The next thing to go was the relationship with my father, Bob. He had always been there for me. He took me in at thirteen years old when no one else would, and he treated me like a son. Hell, I was his son! When I first got into wrestling, he had moved clear across the country to help support me. He was more than just my father; he was also my best friend. But that was a part of the problem. Certain people in my life were envious of the relationship that we had, and now that I only spent a few days at home each month, that envy reached a boiling point. Blockades were thrown up between my father and me; things were said, and the end result was wounded pride. My father and I are alike in many ways, and one of our similarities is stubbornness. Those blockades wouldn't have been hard to break down, but at the time they seemed to be made of stone.

In order to cope with all the stresses in my life, I started doing what the majority of the wrestlers did—lived up the nightlife while on the road. When I first went to the WWF, I steered well away from it. As a matter of fact, I found it almost shocking to learn that some of the wrestlers partied as hard as they did. I remember a few weeks after I had joined, I was in a car with a bunch of my fellow wrestlers heading to a show and one of the guys was lit out of his mind. I nudged the wrestler next to me and said, "What's up with him?"

"Don't worry about it; he does it all the time."

I had done my share of partying when I was younger, but for the past couple of years it was all about hard-core training. I thought the guy was crazy, that it was only a matter of time before he lost his job, but as the weeks started to pass, I began to realize that a lot of wrestlers partied just like him. Some took painkillers to soothe their raging joints, and others dove into a bottle to quell the pain in their back. And there was plenty of pain to go around. I thought I would be giving my body a break going into professional wrestling, but I was wrong. I got more injuries while on the road with the WWF than I ever did in my fighting career. Back, neck, joints—everything was in pain.

After a while I started to wonder how the guys who'd been doing it for ten or fifteen years hung in there. I was having trouble moving around, trouble getting out of bed. I was searching for a way to hang on, so I began doing what all the other guys were doing. I started a dismal routine that allowed me to forget about the pain for a little while. And

once you start that routine, it's easy to get going in a hurry.

I'd get to my hotel late, unable to sleep, so I'd head down to the bar to get a drink. One drink turned into four, and then I was lit. I'd head back to my room, fall into bed, wake up at six in the morning, drive two hours to the next town, work out, eat, do the show, drive two hours back to the hotel, sit down in the bar, have four drinks, then head back up to the room to begin the madness all over again.

I couldn't have managed such a feat while fighting because I would have gotten my head knocked off in the ring. In the WWF, however, my opponents were supposed to protect my body. That didn't always happen, but such matters were out of my hands. If my opponent was tired from the night before and dropped me on my head, there was nothing I could do about it. To put the matches over with the crowd, you couldn't play defense. If my opponent was preparing to bash me over the head with a steel chair, I couldn't put my arm up to block it. I couldn't punch him in the gut so he couldn't land the blow. I had to close my eyes and hope for the best. Each wrestling match was a battle, but you didn't have to be in top physical shape because it was a fake battle. That made all the difference in the world. It made it possible to go out and party every night and still put a match over.

In addition to being beat up and depressed about my home life, I wasn't thrilled about how my character in the WWF was progressing. I was getting a tremendous push, don't get me wrong, but originally Vince had intended to market me as a real action hero. I thought the idea was awesome, and I don't know why Vince didn't follow through with it.

Raising Ortiz's hand after a difficult battle in UFC 40.

Perhaps it was because it took me a little while to find my niche and get comfortable in the ring, I don't know. All I knew was that my character wasn't heading in the direction that we originally discussed. I was extremely popular with the fans, so popular that the WCW marketed Bill Goldberg around my character. His character was almost an exact replica of mine. He was supposed to be a shoot fighter. He had the same facial expressions, and he stopped on the stairs and shook his head like a madman just before he climbed into the ring. He won a few matches and lost a few matches, just like I did. But when promoters realized he was getting over with the fans, he was suddenly unbeatable. I have the highest respect for him because he could certainly carry a show, but I also felt that I could have done an equally good job

with a similar opportunity. After all, I really was a shoot fighter.

Instead of elevating my character to the next level, the WWF brought in Dan Severn. I wasn't sure what Vince was trying to accomplish by doing that because he didn't tell me much about it. So they brought him in. Whatever, it's a business. I knew it was a business. I didn't know if I was going to put him over or he was going to put me over. It didn't really matter. I was getting paid. I didn't, however, feel that it was the wisest decision, because I didn't think Severn was going to get over with the fans.

I learned that I was right when it came time for our first match. I was standing by the Gorilla Station, which is where you have to wait before making your entrance into the arena, and Severn was already down in the ring. He was bouncing around, slapping his chest, and then all of a sudden he takes off his shirt and his belly flops over his trunks. He was fat, sloppy fat. Vince was sitting ringside, watching the action, and over the microphone I heard him tell the referee that Dan had to put his shirt back on. I had to bite my tongue to keep from bursting out in laughter.

So I was standing there watching the monitor, waiting to see how Severn would react, and the referee suddenly cracked a smile. I could tell he too was trying not to burst out laughing. When he gathered his composure, he headed over to Severn and whispered something to him. Severn got this truly perplexed looked on his face, then he shrugged his shoulders, walked back to his corner, and put his shirt back on.

Less than a minute later, I got my name called, and I went down and did a match with him. It was horrible, absolutely terrible. He had no charisma or big moves. Luckily, I didn't get stuck doing matches with him for months and months because he got the boot. He didn't get canned because he was a bad guy; Severn is actually a really nice guy. It's just that he didn't get over with the fans.

I was getting over with the fans. I felt like I could have taken my character further than I did, but that's the way the cookie crumbles. I was making good money, and I was very fortunate to have been given the opportunities that I had. But everything started adding up—the breakdown of the Lion's Den, the barrier between my father and me, the slow

demise of my marriage, the time away from my kids, all the bumps and bruises, and the many late nights sucking down beers. I desperately needed to put my personal life back together, but the only way I could do that was to take a break.

As it turned out, I got what I wanted, but in the worst possible way. I got injured. I was doing a match with Chris Jericho and Curtis Hughes, and Hughes kicked me in the back of the head, stiffed me pretty good. I told him to stay away from the head, and then he stiffed me a second time. I got mad, went after him in the ring for real, but Jericho pulled me off him, told me that he would watch my back. When I went backstage, I could already feel my neck tightening up, and that upset me, so I went up to Hughes and popped him in the mouth. I wasn't trying to knock him out; I just wanted to let him know that what he had done was messed up.

"I just got back," he said. "I haven't been working in a while. I'm sorry."

"Well, next time stay off the head and go to the shoulder."

I hadn't been with the organization all that long, but I did know that when your timing is off, you throw your shots to the body instead of the head. As it turned out, his kicks pinched a nerve in my neck, so I had to go through rehab. The doctors were worried that if I continued to wrestle, the problem would only get worse, so taking some time off was mandatory. The accepted time limit to be away from the WWF was sixty days, and when I still hadn't returned when those sixty days were up, Vince released me from my contract.

9

Rock Bottom

WHEN I GOT OUT OF THE WWF, MY LIFE was a wreck. My wife and I had grown so far apart while I was on the road that there was no hope of saving the marriage, and my father and I were still not speaking. In addition to this, I was also broke. I thought I had put the right people in charge of my finances when I hit the road, but when I went to my bank account to see how much I had, there was nothing. I had to pay taxes, and I didn't have the money. I lost my house, my gym—everything. After fighting all over the world, entertaining thousands upon thousands of fans on a nightly basis, I didn't have a penny to show for it. I was in my mid-thirties and back to square one.

I had every intention of going back to MMA competition when I left the WWF, but I had wanted to take some time to heal and brush up on all my skills. After all, it had been four and a half years since I had slapped on a submission hold with full force. But with bills to pay and mouths to feed, I had to get right down to business. Luckily, I was still a hot commodity when it came to real fighting, thanks to all my fans. I signed the biggest fight deal of my life with the Pride Fighting Championship over in Japan. Pride was pretty much the superbowl of mixed martial arts competition. They routinely sold

out sixty-thousand-seat arenas, and from what I'd heard they were a great company to work for.

I was scheduled to fight Alexander Otsuka, a crafty Japanese competitor, on May 1, 2000, but by the time my neck healed to the point that I could actually get back in the gym and train, I was six weeks out from the fight. Normally that would have been plenty of time to prepare for battle, but I was trying to come back after a four-year layoff.

To get the most out of the little time I had left, I trained in Dallas with Guy Mezger. I didn't have one good week. It was no fault of the guys who had come out to help me prepare; they all did a wonderful job. My body just conked out on me. After taking so much time off, it rejected all the hard-core training. If my muscles weren't cramping up, then my joints were sore. If my joints weren't sore, then my knee would get injured. My body kept shouting, "What the hell is going on here!" It just wasn't used to taking all that pounding anymore.

Two weeks before the fight, I knew I wasn't in the best of shape. I started to get a little concerned, but once I stepped into the ring in front of thirty thousand fight fans, all doubt washed away. That's just the way my mind works when it comes to fighting. I'm confident; I've always been confident. On occasion I've been confident when I probably shouldn't have been, mainly due to injuries, but it's not something I can turn off. I could have two broken legs, and I would still think I could walk through anyone. I realize now how such thinking can bite you in the ass, but that wasn't the case with Otsuka. We took the battle all over the ring, down to the canvas and then back up to the feet, but I dominated Otsuka the entire time. And when I had him gassed, I nailed him with a flurry of punches and knocked him out cold.

My next fight in Pride, held August 27, 2000, didn't go so well. I was determined to get the kind of training that I needed this time, but just as I was gearing up to fly out to Dallas and train with the boys, my wife dropped our four kids off at my place and then left town. I was staying in a small apartment, and since my father and I still weren't talking, I had no one to help me with the kids. I wasn't comfortable putting my children in the hands of a babysitter I didn't know, so it made things tough. I was taking the kids to school and to their baseball games. I was helping them with their homework. Spending time with my kids was wonderful, but my training suffered. Not able to go to Dallas for obvious reasons, I searched all over town for a place to train but had no luck. Backing out of the fight would have been the best option, but there was no way I could do that—I was the main draw. So I did the only thing I could do; I spent time with my kids and hoped for the best.

When I started warming up backstage on the night of the fight, I remember already getting tired. The event was outdoors, and it was hot and humid. I was just doing some light grappling, but I could already feel my gas start to run low. I thought to myself, "Well, let's just see what happens."

I actually did quite well with only seven days of serious training under my belt. My opponent was Kazuyuki Fugita, a big, burly Japanese fighter who liked to take his opponents to the ground and then beat them into oblivion. Fugita tried that on several occasions, but he couldn't take me down. I beat on him from one side of the ring to the other for the first couple of minutes, even knocked him to his back. The reason I didn't pounce on top of him once I did knock him down was because I was too damn tired. When I train properly for a fight, I don't get tired in the ring. I can go through anything. For the first time in my life, however, that wasn't the case.

That realization became very clear when Fugita trapped me up against the ropes. He was also tired, and neither of us was doing anything. We were just standing there, holding on to each other. I might have appeared fine to everyone in attendance—after all, I had been dominating the fight up to that point—but inside I was a mess. My heart felt like it was about to tear out of my chest, and I kept getting white flashes across my vision. I was about to drop, and I knew it. Instead of doing that, I looked over to my corner and told them to throw in the towel.

I told myself that my next fight in Pride was going to be the one where I brought out the old Ken Shamrock, the guy who had dominated the competition for all those years in the Octagon and the rings of Pancrase. My next opponent was going to be Igor Vovchanchin, a very dangerous Russian kickboxer who could put me in a whole lot of pain if I wasn't on top of my game. I set aside the training time and cleared my mind of any thought that didn't concern

Kimo struggles to regain consciousness after I knocked him to his backside with a powerful knee to the face in UFC 48.

the fight. Then I got busy. Less than a month into this mad training binge, however, I injured my neck. I sucked up the pain and worked through it, just as I always did. Then, two weeks later, I tore the anterior cruciate ligament (ACL) in my knee.

The ACL injury was a little more serious, something I couldn't just grit my teeth and plow through. I knew fighting Vovchanchin was out of the question, but there was a more serious issue at hand—would I ever be able to fight again? I went to one doctor, and he told me that I needed surgery. I didn't want surgery because I was afraid that I would never recover, so I went to another doctor and he told me the exact same thing. Still not satisfied with the answer, I went to a third doctor. He also said that I needed surgery, but he did propose an alternative. He said that he

could put me on a rehabilitation program to strengthen my hamstring and calf muscles. It wouldn't give me very good mobility in the ring, but at least I could get to a point where I could fight.

So I started to strengthen my hamstring and calf muscles. About a year later, I signed a contract to fight Don Frye in Pride on February 24, 2002. My knee was in just as bad shape as it had been when I tore my ACL, but I was too darn stubborn to admit that my injury was serious. I thought I could work through it just as I had in the old days. And besides, I really, really wanted to fight Frye, especially after the trash talking began. He claimed that I had ducked him back at the Ultimate Ultimate, which was complete garbage. I have never ducked a fight in my life, and I never will. Then he got more personal. He knew my dad and I weren't on speaking terms at the moment, and he started saying that he was going to have my father work his corner for the fight. I realized that the relationship between my father and me wasn't the best at that particular moment, but he was still my father. He is the best man I have ever known, and there was no way he would ever do that to me, not in a million years. So that pissed me off, made it personal. I understood that Frye was trying to hype up our battle, get some controversy going, but I'm a firm believer that you never involve family.

You can bet I trained for that one. I worked out in Dallas for two solid months, and I got in some good sessions. I still only had full mobility in one leg, which meant that taking the fight to the ground would be next to impossible, but I didn't care. I climbed into the ring with Frye and did the best I could under the circumstances, and it was actually a very entertaining fight. We went toe to toe, both landing some good shots, and then he caught me with a wicked punch and knocked me out. When I woke up, I was still fighting. I had somehow taken Frye to the ground and caught him in a heel hook. I had been fighting for so long, it was all an involuntary response.

I cranked on his heel hard—hard enough to feel ligaments popping underneath his skin—but Frye was a tough competitor and refused to tap. When the bout fell into the hands of the judges, I was confident that I had won. Frye had knocked me down, but I had hooked his heel. As it turned out, the judges didn't feel the same as I did. It was a split descision in Frye's favor.

After that fight, I seriously considered retiring—never in my life had I lost two fights in a row. My

contract with Pride was up, so I took a little time to try and sort out my personal life. Truth be told, I didn't have much to sort out. There was nothing in my apartment to come home to, so I started staying out later and later. After a while of that, I wanted to get things back in order, and I thought the best way to do that was to take on another fight. I wanted to come back to the UFC. I thought that it might rekindle some of that fire I'd had back in the old days when Royce and I were hunting for each other's head. And I had the perfect opponent to get me charged up—Tito Ortiz.

There had been some bad blood between the two of us ever since he'd squared of with Guy Mezger in UFC 19, held on March 5, 1999. Ortiz had won the fight by a referee's stoppage, but it was certainly a questionable stop. It was late in the fight and both of them were completely gassed. Guy was balled up on his elbows and knees. Tito was on top of him, throwing punches to the back of his head. At this point in the UFC, they had made punches to the back of the head illegal. The referee didn't pick up on that, fine. But they were not the type of punches that you end a fight on. They had absolutely nothing behind them. The referee kept asking Guy if he was fine, and Guy kept nodding his head, telling him "Yes, I'm fine." And then the referee ended the bout.

I didn't agree with the decision, but I wasn't about to hop in the ring and protest. There was a time and place for everything, and once the tournament was over, I would let my voice be heard. So I figured that was it, the fight was over. Both fighters put out tremendous heart, and now it was time to shake hands. That was not what happened. Instead of meeting Guy in the ring and showing his respect,

Tito puts on a T-shirt that read GAY MEZGER IS MY BITCH. Then, to top off his insult, he flips off our corner, the Lion's Den corner, with both hands.

I just came unglued. I was in the WWF at the time, but my heart was still with the UFC. The moment Tito put on that T-shirt, I remembered all the hard work I had put into helping get the UFC where it was. I remembered all those times when people said that we were nothing but animals, and that we should be locked up in prison. All of us who were involved in the early years had put forth a tremendous amount of effort to keep the sport from getting banned, to prove its critics wrong, and then to have someone like Tito come out there and disrespect the event and my group of fighters like that—I came unglued.

From that day forth, the animosity built and built. Tito challenged me at one point, but I was in the WWF at the time and he knew there was no way I could accept. As soon as I got released from my WWF contract, I had tried to come to the UFC, but they didn't want to pay what I thought I was worth, and Pride did. Now, however, was a different matter. I wanted to fight Tito in the worst possible way.

There was only one small problem—I still had a bum knee. I wanted to fight Tito so bad that I convinced myself that I could beat him with all my injuries. I actually convinced myself that I could beat him with one good leg. Without the ability to shoot in for his legs, I was pretty limited in what I could do in the ring. I figured that I could still knock him out, so that is what I focused on. I started working real hard on boxing and defending against takedowns. If he managed to take me to the ground, then I planned to get back up. That was

going to be hard to do with a bad knee, simply because it would effect my base and balance, but in training I worked on escaping from the bottom position using one leg.

Training didn't start off on a good foot due to the fact that most days I had to call it quits by noon because of complications with my knee, but things only got worse. Tito was fighting as a light heavyweight, which meant that I had to get down to 205 pounds. I weighed 225 pounds when I started my program, but the weight wasn't coming off as fast as normal because I couldn't run. Every time I tried to run, my bad knee would swell up like a balloon. I remember ten days prior to the fight I was still ten pounds over. I started freaking out because that was a whole lot of weight to drop in ten days, so I crashed my diet and ended up getting down to 200 pounds. I looked in pretty damn good shape, but the weight loss had zapped my energy.

Despite feeling lethargic and only having use of one leg, I felt that I could still beat Tito Ortiz. That's how hardheaded I can be. I had lost my fight with Fugita, lost my fight with Frye, and still I hadn't learned my lesson. It wasn't until Tito and I actually started fighting that I realized just how large my handicap was. I couldn't shoot, and I couldn't land submissions because I needed both legs to get into position and help lock in holds. I also couldn't turn my punches over because my bad knee kept my body from pivoting. So there were a lot of things hindering me from doing what I needed to do. As a result, I got beat. I took that fight knowing that I was hurt, thinking that I would be able to overcome the obstacles in my way, and I paid the consequences. Tito was better prepared, and I got beat by a better fighter.

10 Lessons Learned

IN MANY WAYS IT WAS GOOD THAT I DIDN'T WIN the Tito fight because I learned a lot from the loss. I learned that I was approaching forty and that I could no longer look past my injuries. I couldn't behave as if I were still twenty-five years old. I had to work harder, train smarter, and do whatever it took to get healthy, both mentally and physically. So that is what I did. I started by contacting my father, and, being the exceptional man that he is, he welcomed me back with open arms. Then I arranged to have surgery on my bum knee. I didn't know if I would be able to fight after the surgery, or if even if I would be able to walk, but there was only one way to find out.

A couple of weeks before I was to throw my knee up on the chopping block, I received a phone call from a woman I had fallen in love with twenty-seven years before. I had met her just a few days after I had first arrived at my father's group home. One of the kids in the home was having a birthday. My father had invited over a couple of his friends, and they had brought their daughter, Tonya. I was thirteen years old, a hotheaded young scrapper, and she knocked me out with a one-two combination that I never saw coming. When she walked by me, I said under my breath, "I'm going to marry that girl." As it turned out, I hadn't said it as lightly as I hoped—both her and her parents had heard me, and her parents still tease her about it to this day.

After our first meeting I never took my eyes off her, not for the next five years. I didn't ask girls out back then because I wasn't all that good with words, so I ended up dating a slew of cheerleaders who were eager to go out with the high school rebel. When I finally got the nerve up to ask her out when she was seventeen, she was already seriously involved with someone else. But she was still there for me. I remember when I broke my neck and was strapped to my bed, she used to come by and hold my hand. And when she was in trouble, I was always there for her. This one time, the guy she was dating got a little out of line, and her father came and told me about it. I was hell-bent on killing the guy, but somehow Tonya talked me out of it. I knew she liked me, and she knew that I liked her. We were just dumb kids who loved each other but didn't know how to bring that love together.

One of the worst days of my life was when Tonya got married. My family had grown close to her family over the years, and we wanted her special day to be as special as possible, so my father and I decided to have her wedding reception at our house. I helped set up things around the house, get everything prepared, but when it came time to head over to the chapel to see her united in holy matrimony, I refused to go. I stopped by the reception briefly to wish her a good life, but then I skipped out. It was just too painful to see her wearing the ring of another man.

We kept in touch over the years, even made it a point to see each other whenever we were both in Susanville, but we made sure to keep these visits brief. The flames of passion were still there, still lurking in the back of both of our minds, and we were both married and had our own paths ahead of us.

That, however, was no longer the case.

When we talked on the phone, we discussed our children—she had three and I had four. We talked about old times. As we did this, we realized we were both still very much in love. We didn't come right out and say it, but some things don't need to be said. Two days later she flew down to San Diego, which was where I had moved while wrestling in the WWF, and we have been together ever since.

For the first time in a long time I had a reason to come home at night. I had Tonya, the love of my life, seven wonderful children, and my father all under one roof. The desolate rooms of my home suddenly filled up with laughter, conversation, and arguments, and never had I been so happy. There was a lot of responsibility, but even with all the kids' football games, baseball games, and track meets—even with all the bickering, dentist appointments, and doctor appointments—my fight training actually started to get better. I started to acquire the fire that I'd had when hunting for Royce in the early years of the UFC. I began to feel hungry again.

I got my knee surgery, and two weeks later I was running laps around the track. The doctor couldn't believe how quickly I healed, nor could I. I kicked myself for not doing it sooner. In a matter of just a couple of months, I could shoot in again, do all the things that had once made me such a feared and respected fighter. As a matter of fact, I was even adding new techniques to my repertoire. After my fight with Tito, Joe Rogan, an announcer at the UFC, commented on how I had been training with the same guys for fifteen years, and how if I wanted to get better, I had to switch things up. At first I took it as an insult. My guys are the toughest warriors on the planet; they are like a family to me. They had always been there for me, always. But then I took a step back, thought about it, and realized there was some truth to what he said. So I started making some changes. I began training with Eric Paulson, an experienced shoot fighter, as well as several boxing coaches. They gave me an entirely new outlook on training. They brought in different bodies to spar with, and it put me on my toes, made me sharp again.

The only thing I needed now was to get a fight, so I contacted Dana White, the president of the UFC. He brought up Tank Abbott, and immediately my eyes lit up. We'd had many run-ins over the years; yet we had never met in the cage. I thought it would be a great fight, and the UFC thought it would be a great fight. They sent the contracts over, I signed them, and then I dove into training. Not long later, Tank started with his usual song and dance, telling reporters how he had been waiting to put his hands on me for years, how he was going to knock me out and do all sorts of nasty things. I didn't bother to reply—I was going to do my talking in the ring.

Two weeks after I signed the contracts, however, I got a call from White.

Back on top after my victory over Kimo in UFC 48.

"Hey, brother, I've got some bad news," he said.

"What's up?"

"Well, I can't seem to get in touch with Tank. He was calling me two or three times a week for the past couple of months, but now I can't get a hold of him. He's disappeared."

"You have no way of getting in touch with him?"

"He won't call me back."

"What do you want to do?"

"Unless Tank calls me and signs the contract, it looks like we have to give you someone else. Is there anyone you have in mind?"

"Give me somebody, I don't care," I said. "I just want to get in there and fight."

I should have known that Tank would never have fought me. In any case, Kimo stepped up. He wanted revenge since our first encounter, and I thought it would be a good fight. Besides, he had beaten Tank in the last event, so when I beat Kimo, I figured I would be killing two birds with one stone.

While warming up backstage on the night of the fight, my mind was clear and focused. I didn't have to worry about where my kids were, my knee was back to normal, and, having given up the nightlife, I had gotten the training that I needed to win. I was at 95 percent of my former self, ready for an all-out war.

It didn't turn out to be much of a war, but I was certainly happy with my performance. Shortly after the bout began, Kimo rushed forward, threw a punch that grazed my face, and then tied me up in the clinch. Ever since I had beaten him back in UFC 8, he had been studying Brazilian jujitsu. I guess he thought he was good enough to finish me off with a submission hold because his reason for tying me up in the clinch was to take me to the ground. But Ken Shamrock is not an easy competitor to take down, as Kimo quickly learned. Tied up in the clinch, he bull-dogged me from one corner of the Octagon to the other, trying to throw off my balance. When my balance remained keen, he tried to drop low for a take-down. Instead of snatching my legs, however, he ate a knee to the forehead. It didn't knock him out, but it certainly rattled his bell.

He was strong, but then so was I. And the clinch was nothing new to me. I had been pummeling with opponents since I was thirteen years old. Instead of playing a game of tug-of-war with Kimo, I worked on bettering my position in the clinch. While he focused on trying to take me down, I slipped both arms underneath his arms and attempted to clasp my hands together behind his back. Once I achieved that, I would have the leverage to suck Kimo's body into mine and then dump him onto his back—I would have the leverage to do all sorts of nasty things.

Kimo wasn't about to wait around for that to happen, so as I was trying to clasp my hands together behind his back, he attempted to back out of the clinch. While he did this, I kept upward pressure on his arms, forcing him to duck his head to escape. And the moment he ducked his head, I brought up a thunderous knee to his jaw, knocking him out cold.

Just before the fight, the fans had been split—some of them had cheered for Kimo, and some of them had cheered for me. But now that Kimo was lying on his back, his eyes rolled back into his head, it was amazing how many of them were thrilled about my victory. I had earned back their trust after my poor performance with Tito, and they were glad to see that The World's Most Dangerous Man was back. I was excited about what I had just accomplished, excited to see that my knee could endure the test of battle, but at the same time it wasn't a huge deal for me. In the back of my mind, it wasn't all that satisfying. The world didn't come to an end with that one fight—I had so much more to accomplish. I needed to get the Lion's Den back in order, and I needed to start training for my next fight. At forty years old, I only had a few years left of battle. If I was going to make the most of those years, there could be no time for celebration.

So that is where I am at now. I'm getting bigger, stronger, and meaner than ever. When I'm not coaching football and wrestling at my kids' high school, taking walks with my wonderful wife, or spending time with my father, I'm in the gym training. I'm learning how to be a smarter fighter, and I'm also learning how to be a smarter husband and father.

PART TWO
The Art of Submission Fighting

11

Submission Fighting

SUBMISSION FIGHTING IS A SYSTEM OF hand-to-hand combat designed for the street and mixed martial arts (MMA) competition. It is not based on a bunch of flashy punches and kicks, but rather techniques that have proven successful time and again in fighting tournaments where there are few to no rules of engagement. It is not the easiest martial art to learn. It involves hundreds of hours hefting opponents off their feet and slamming them to the ground, locking in submission holds with bone-breaking pressure, and fighting while lying on your back. It involves learning how to weather a storm of punches and escape from agonizing chokeholds. It involves thousands of sit-ups and pull-ups and squats. It's a martial art designed specifically for men and women who have the heart and desire to learn how to fight.

So if you have come looking for a martial art where you can judge your fighting ability by the color of belt wrapped around your waist, you have come to the wrong place. In my training camp, the Lion's Den, students do not wear colored belts because it will not help them win a fight. If you have come looking for a martial art where you get to wear a uniform, you will need to look elsewhere. In my camp we do not study Brazilian jujitsu—we don't

base our sweeps, setups, or submission holds on grabbing on to an opponent's uniform because out in the street clothes rip and tear and in the rings of the MMA competitors are seldom allowed to wear a uniform. If you have come looking for a martial art that teaches you how to deal with the unpredictability of real combat and learn how to gain the upper hand in any fighting situation, then you have found the right doorstep.

In the Lion's Den, we build champions through hard training and effective technique. Unlike many of the training camps that were around when the sport of MMA first burst onto the scene, we have stayed on the top tier of competition because we constantly evolve, constantly throw out old techniques that no longer work and create or adopt new ones that do. For a while Brazilian jujitsu was the popular style, but more and more competitors have been moving over to submission fighting because they realize that real fights are seldom like grappling matches. Without uniforms to soak up the sweat, bodies slip and slide. Having precise technique is definitely a must, but you also need to know how to scramble for position. Submission fighters thrive off the scramble; it is what we do best. When we can't lock in a submission on our opponent's arm, we change positions so we can attack his leg. When we can't sink in a submission on his leg, we escape back to our feet. When we can't get a knockout on our feet, we get a takedown and obtain a dominant position on the ground. Fighting is about creating options, and if you learn the techniques I have shared in the following pages, you will have plenty of them.

There's no need to go out and hit the weight room before you start your education. I happen to be a muscular guy, and I use my size well. But that's not true for everyone. If you spend all your time power lifting and bulking up, it is often going to be more difficult to strike and move your body on the ground. It's going to take more energy to do every-thing. And if you haven't complemented your strength training with cardio training, you'll most likely run out of gas in the first round. If you practice the techniques in each of the upcoming sections, flowing from one position to the next with your training partner, you will garner dynamic strength, which is the kind of strength you're going to need for battle. It'll allow you to march through a fight for long periods of time and be explosive when opportunities present themselves. So if you are interested in learning the art of submission fighting, there's no time like the present. You're going to need a pair of shorts and perhaps a pair of kneepads. All the rest is heart and desire.

12

Striking

WITH NEARLY EVER MMA FIGHTER NOW versed in both the standing phase and ground phase of combat, the sport has become more competitive than ever. You can no longer be just a striker or just a grappler. If you focus exclusively on grappling and go up against a master striker who has learned to defend the takedown, there is a good chance that you're going to get knocked out. If you focus exclusively on striking and go up against a proficient grappler, there's a good chance you'll end up on your back before landing your knockout shot. To be a complete fighter, you're going to have to be proficient in both phases of combat, and getting your strikes up to par is a good place to start. You don't need to have the hands of Mohammad Ali or the legs of a Muay Thai kickboxer, but you definitely have to know how to punch and kick. The techniques I have laid out in the following section will get you started, but once you have them down, you will need to work on putting them together in combinations. If you are looking for a knockout, as you should be, combinations are the way to get it.

■ Stance

Although there are literally hundreds of different fighting stances in the martial arts, relatively few of them work well for MMA competition. The one that seems to work best for the majority of competitors, whether they consider themselves primarily grapplers or primarily strikers, is the basic stance from Muay Thai kickboxing.

I'll put you in the stance from the bottom up, so start by placing your feet side by side a shoulder's width apart and letting your arms dangle at your sides. The first thing you want to do is move your right foot a few inches back so that if you were to draw a horizontal line between your legs, the toes of your right foot would be just behind the line while the heel of your left foot would be just in front of it. Once you get your feet in place, you want to come up slightly on the balls of your feet. It doesn't have to be much, just a few centimeters, but it is important that you distribute your weight equally on the balls of both feet. Standing flat-footed will not only make it more difficult to move, but it will also rob power from your punches and kicks.

Next, slightly bend your knees. It is important that your never lock your knees while in the standing position, ever. You don't have to bend them dramatically; it could be such a slight bend that it's hardly noticeable to the eye. Just don't lock them straight. If you do, you won't have the mobility

A roundhouse kick targeting your opponent's neck.

An uppercut targeting your opponent's chin.

A knee or front kick targeting your opponent's sternum.

A front roundhouse kick targeting your opponent's ribs.

A roundhouse kick targeting your opponent's ribs.

An outside knee targeting your opponent's ribs.

A front kick targeting your opponent's lead hip.

A front roundhouse kick targeting your opponent's rear thigh.

A roundhouse kick targeting the meat of your opponent's thigh.

An inside leg kick targeting the inside of your opponent's thigh just below his groin.

A roundhouse kick underneath your opponent's check, targeting his rear calf.

Fighting Stance

Eyes on your opponent.

Chin tucked.

Back slightly arched.

Elbows tucked tightly into your body.

Hips facing toward your opponent.

Groin slightly pressed out.

Knees slightly bent.

Toes of your rear foot lined up with the heel of your lead foot.

Weight evenly distributed on the balls of your feet.

Feet spaced a shoulder's width apart.

needed to kick, punch, or defend a takedown. You might also end up with a broken leg.

Moving up the body, you want to turn your hips so that they are facing your opponent. It might feel natural to turn your hips more to the side, which is permissible to a degree, especially out on the street where there are no rules prohibiting groin strikes. But by turning your hips to the side you're going to lose power in your roundhouse kicks and your ability to check your opponent's kicks. If you're going up against a fighter who throws hard kicks to the leg, keep your hips front and center.

With your hips facing the front, thrust your groin out just a little and tighten the muscles in your buttocks. This will allow you to be explosive with your kicks on a moment's notice, as well as successfully check your opponent's kicks.

Now that your lower body is taken care of, bring your hands up to protect your face. There are a lot of MMA competitors who keep their hands low so they can defend against a takedown, but there are also a lot of competitors who get knocked out by doing this. If you need to defend against a takedown, it doesn't take much effort to reposition your hands, so the safe bet is to keep them up at least at chin level. Next, tuck your arms tightly against your sides to protect your ribs. You also want to tuck your chin toward your chest. It might feel natural to keep your chin high to show that you're confident, but if you're fighting a kickboxer, it's a good way to end up with a broken neck.

Once you have gotten all of your body parts into place, you're ready to start moving around. You might find it difficult at first to maintain a proper stance, especially when an opponent is throwing bombs at you, so you should make it a habit while sparring to constantly check your positioning. If your chin is up or your legs are spread too far apart, fix the problem. By constantly correcting your mistakes, you'll keep them from becoming instinctual.

■ Movement

Movement is the key to having good offense and defense while fighting on your feet, so let's get right to the meat and potatoes, starting with moving from side to side. If you are inside striking range, there are several rules you must always follow. The first and most important of these rules is to never cross your feet. If you do, you're going to be vulnerable to virtually every attack in the book for the split second that it takes you to uncross them. So, if you want to move to your left, step with your left leg first. Once it touches ground in the new location, drag your right foot along so that you can reacquire your proper stance. Your steps should not be big steps because that would violate your second rule while in striking distance—never get too stretched out. If you need to cover a large distance in a short amount of time, do not take a giant step with your leg, plant your foot, and then drag the other leg up. Instead you should use a lunge, which can be a little tricky to learn. If you want to cover a large distance to your left, you're going to push your body off the ball of your right foot. When in a proper fighting stance, this shouldn't be hard to do. The tricky part is not getting stretched out. You don't want to wait for your left foot to land before you bring up your right foot. Your right foot needs to come off the ground with your left, so it is almost like you're maintaining a proper fighting stance while both feet skim along the canvas to your new position. When learning this technique, a lot of students will try to skip instead of lunge, or when moving to their left side, they'll push off their left foot instead of their right. Getting it right can take some time, and there are some important things you should keep in mind while practicing. First, the lunge is not an upward motion, but rather a motion that carries your body on the most direct route to your new location. Second, do not widen your stance to get a better lunge. In order to use this technique during a fight, you must be able to do it from a regular fighting stance.

Moving from side to side outside your opponent's striking range is a lot simpler. You can employ either of the tactics above or simply shuffle from side to side. Shuffling works great when an opponent is trying to box you into the corner of the cage or ring, because you can quickly circle around him and work back out into open ground. It is important when you do this, however, never to cross your feet or turn your hips away from your opponent. There are competitors out there who can cover large distances in a short amount of time, so you need to be able to drop back into your fighting stance before your opponent can come within striking range.

Moving forward and back while inside striking range has the same rules as moving from side to side when in striking range. You don't want to cross your feet, and you don't want to get too spread out. If you want to move forward, step with your lead leg first; if you want to move backward, step with your rear leg first. The lunge also works particularly well, but because your intentions for moving forward or back will most likely be to strike or avoid your opponent's strikes, you really need to have this technique down pat.

Now that you understand *how* to move, lets focus a little on where, when, and why you should move. Moving backward can often save your hide when an opponent advances upon you in a flurry, but it's not going to better your situation. If you get your body moving backward at a rapid pace, you're going to have very little offense. It's going to be hard to punch or kick or shoot for a takedown because you won't have a solid base from which to garner power for your attack. And if your opponent is fast enough, he just might be able to overrun your retreat, which is exactly what Vitor Belfort did to Wanderlei Silva in Ultimate Brazil, held on October 16, 1998. While backpedaling, Silva got hit with half a dozen or more firm punches, and when the Octagon fence stopped his backward motion, his situation got much worse.

For these reasons, it is much wiser to move from side to side when an opponent comes blazing forward with an attack. In order for your opponent to continue with his assault, he will now have to redirect his attack to whichever side you moved to. By that time, you will have already launched an attack of your own, performed a takedown, or moved a safe distance away. Breaking your natural instinct to retreat linearly is not easily achieved, but it is worth putting time and effort into because it can make all the difference between victory and defeat. Fighting on your feet is not about who can throw the hardest punch or kick, it's about finesse, working your body into a position where you can administer a beating without the risk of getting one back.

A more subtle movement you can employ is the fake. You see this a lot in boxing, but it works even better in MMA competition because there are a lot more things to fake than just punches. You can fake shooting for a takedown to get your opponent to drop his hands and open up for a punch. You can fake a punch to force your opponent to raise his hands so you can shoot for a takedown. You can fake a jab to open you up for a kick, or vice versa. The options are limitless, but there are a few rules you need to go by no matter which fake you are trying to employ. First, you must never commit too much of your balance. A fake is just that, a fake. There is no chance of hurting your opponent with the fake alone, so there is no reason to make yourself vulnerable in the process. When trying to fake a jab, don't commit your weight to your lead leg like you are really going to throw the jab. If your opponent is a skilled competitor, he'll be reading your attacks by watching your hips. If your hips make a sudden jerk to the right, he'll know that you're either going to throw a jab or a kick with your front leg, and usually that will be enough to get your desired response out of him. When trying to fake a cross, don't extend your body forward. A quick jerk of your hips to the left will usually be enough. And whenever you do fake a move, be prepared for retaliation, because that will most likely be your opponent's response.

The last thing I will leave you with as far as movement is to do it as much as possible. Standing in one spot and playing tough guy is not the way to win a fight. Proper movement will create angles, and angles are your ticket to the knockout.

■ Punching

If you approach MMA competition as if it were a boxing match, you're going to be in trouble. You can certainly employ many of the techniques used in boxing, but not everything translates from one sport

to the other. First off, you're not going to be wearing sixteen-ounce boxing gloves. In MMA competition, competitors wear gloves that are only slightly bigger than their hands. One solid punch can send you to La-La Land, so it can be dangerous to do some of those fancy moves that you see in boxing, such as standing directly in front of your opponent with your hands down. I suppose you can, but if your timing is off by even a millisecond, you're going to wake up on a stretcher.

Another luxury boxers have that MMA competitors don't is the use of dramatic bobbing and weaving. It is a great way to steer clear of punches while in striking range, but in MMA competition your opponent's punches aren't all you have to worry about. If your opponent has studied any form of kickboxing, the moment you drop your head too low he will most likely kick it or crash a knee into your face. I'm not saying that you should never bob and weave, but you should definitely get a feel for your opponent's arsenal of strikes before you do. If he seems to like those kicks and knees, I would suggest staying away from the bob and weave and focusing instead on moving from side to side or covering up. But covering up can also be dangerous in MMA competition, as Tito Ortiz learned when he took on Chuck Liddell in UFC 47, held on April 2, 2004. When Liddell advanced with a flurry of punches, Ortiz covered his face with his arms. If he had been wearing sixteen-ounce boxing gloves, his face would have been well protected. As it was, Liddell managed to squeak enough shots around Ortiz's tiny gloves to sink his ship.

So now that you know MMA competition is nothing like boxing, let me pass on a little knowledge that I learned from competition. First and foremost, pick and choose your shots. This also applies when you've got your opponent trapped in a vulnerable position. It can be easy to get carried away, but if one of your punches strays off target, rain can quickly dump on your parade. Recall that I learned this the hard way in the Ultimate Ultimate '96, when I had Brian Johnston lying on his back and trapped up against the fence. I could have worked for a submission hold, but I was in the mood to strike. When my hard right veered a little high and crashed into the side of his head, I caved my knuckle in and had to sit out the rest of the tournament.

So take it from me, choose your shots. Monitor your opponent's movement and pick him apart. Play a careful game, but unload when you see an opening. And don't overcommit. If you try throwing these big haymakers, you'll open yourself up for getting taken to the ground. Last but not least, learn how to grapple. The better you become at defending takedowns and escaping back to your feet when the fight does go to the ground, the more confident you will be at unleashing your hands.

Jab

The jab is an excellent punch, not for its power, but for its versatility. You can use a jab to bloody your opponent's nose, disrupt his balance, or temporarily blind him with your fist so you can launch a more powerful strike such as a right cross or rear roundhouse kick. If you are looking to shoot in for the takedown but your opponent is prepared to defend the takedown, a quick jab will usually redirect his focus to protecting his face. It is important to remember that although it's often difficult to knock your opponent out with a jab, it is still one of your most valuable striking tools.

1 I'm in a fighting stance within striking range of my opponent, preparing to throw the jab. It is important to note that if your opponent is not within striking range, you don't want to lean forward or spread your feet far apart just to land the punch. If you need to cover some distance to connect, push off your rear foot and lunge both legs forward at the same time so you can maintain your fighting stance.

2 Taking a small step forward with my left foot, I turn my hips slightly in a clockwise direction and spin on the ball of my left foot at the same time. As my rotating hips force my shoulders to also turn in a clockwise direction, I lash out nice and straight with my left hand, turning my hand over so that my palm is facing the ground. It is important to note that as I throw the punch I keep my right hand up to guard the right side of my face, my chin remains tucked to my chest, and my left shoulder comes up to protect the left side of my face. I have not overcommitted to the punch, making it easier to draw my hand straight back to my chin.

Cross

If you can land a solid cross to your opponent's jaw, there is a good chance that he'll go down. The main thing you must keep in mind before throwing the cross, however, is that it's not a haymaker. Just as with the jab, you garner power for the strike from your hips. You don't want to muscle the punch. You don't want to draw your fist back. You don't want to loop it out wide, and you don't want to stretch your body out so you can reach your opponent's face. All these things will not only make the cross harder to land, but they will also give your opponent a better chance of connecting with punches of his own. If you fire the punch off your chin, generate power from your hips, and throw your fist straight down the pipe, there's a good chance that the punch will connect.

1 I'm in a fighting stance within striking range of my opponent, preparing to throw the cross.

2 Taking a small step forward with my left foot, I pivot my hips in a counterclockwise direction. As my rotating hips force my shoulders to also turn in a counterclockwise direction, I lash out nice and straight with my right hand, turning my hand over so that my palm is facing the ground. I've kept my left hand guarding the left side of my face, and my right shoulder has come up to protect the right side of my face.

Hook

A lot of people have the perception that a hook is a big looping punch that comes barreling down from the heavens and crashes into their opponent's jaw. If you throw a hook like that in MMA competition, the chances are your opponent will fire a hard cross straight down the middle and knock you out long before your hook has come anywhere close to landing. When done right, the hook is not a dramatic punch, but rather a stealthy one. It is like both the jab and the cross in that you generate power for the blow from your hips. Arching your hand out wide will accomplish nothing more than telegraphing your attack, so it should be fired right off your chin. If you are like most fighters, you will probably find that the hook works best after you've successfully slipped your opponent's jab.

1 I'm in my fighting stance, preparing to throw the hook.

2 As I take a small step to my left with my lead leg, I turn my hips and shoulders slightly in a counterclockwise direction and put a little bend in my knees. This position change should not be dramatic, just enough to wind you up for the punch.

3 I lift my left elbow so that it's level with my shoulder. Keeping my arm bent at a forty-five-degree angle, I snap my hips in a clockwise direction. This snap of my hips carries my fist into the side of Jason's jaw. It should be noted that this strike takes very little effort when done correctly. The more you tighten up and try to muscle the punch, the less steam you will have behind it.

Slipping a Punch

Slipping a punch can be a great way to avoid a shot, but you have to be careful because MMA competition is nothing like a boxing match. If you utilize this technique too much in a fight, your opponent might catch on. Then he might throw a jab, wait for you to slip it, and follow up with a knee or a kick to your head. For this reason, it is important that you don't drop your head too low. It is also important that you try to retaliate as often as possible after slipping a punch. You could throw a punch of your own or go for a takedown. It's important that you do something because if you just keep slipping your opponent's punches and not retaliating, eventually your opponent will pick you apart.

1 I'm in a fighting stance, looking for an opportunity to strike.

2 Jason throws a jab, and I slip it by quickly rotating my hips, shoulders, and head in a clockwise direction. I've kept my head up to avoid a kick or knee to the face, and I've kept my feet in the same spot so I can defend a takedown attempt by sprawling my legs back. This new position sets me up nicely for a takedown, a right hook to Jason's jaw or ribs, or a round kick to Jason's ribs.

3 Jason follows his jab with a cross, and I slip his punch by quickly snapping my hips, shoulders, and head in a counterclockwise direction. This sets me up for a round kick to Jason's lead leg or a left hook to his jaw.

Parrying a Punch

Parrying a punch is a great defensive tool, especially if you're fighting a competitor with a good jab. You can use either your right or left hand to execute the parry; it is all a matter of preference. The trick to becoming effective with this technique is simply practice, having your training partner throw hundreds of jabs at your face so you can learn proper timing. Once you can successfully parry your opponent's jab, you're going to want to work on a quick retaliation with your opposite hand.

1 I'm in a fighting stance, searching for an opening to strike.

2 Jason throws a jab at my face, and I drop my right hand down on top of his punch.

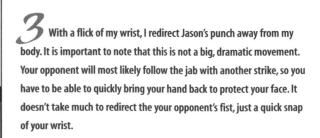

3 With a flick of my wrist, I redirect Jason's punch away from my body. It is important to note that this is not a big, dramatic movement. Your opponent will most likely follow the jab with another strike, so you have to be able to quickly bring your hand back to protect your face. It doesn't take much to redirect the your opponent's fist, just a quick snap of your wrist.

Blocking a Punch

Boxers can use their hands quite effectively to block a punch because they're wearing sixteen-ounce gloves. Their battle mitts practically cover one whole side of their face, as well as provide cushioning for the blow. Competitors in MMA competition don't have that luxury. If you try blocking a punch by putting your tiny glove up against the side of your face, it's going to hurt. If the punch connects with your hand, it will send a shock wave right through your glove and into your ear or jaw. It will probably feel like you didn't have your hand up at all. And if the punch slips around the glove, which is quite likely, the damage will be even worse. So when you have to block a punch in MMA competition, it's better to use your arm and/or elbow. If your opponent's punch connects with your elbow, it is going to hurt him much worse that it hurts you.

1 I'm in a fighting stance, looking for an opening.

2 Jason throws a hard jab. To block the shot, I bring my left arm up and shield the side of my face and head. It is important when doing this to place your protection arm snug against your head. It is also important to immediately launch a strike of your own to prevent your opponent from advancing with a flurry of punches. A good choice would be a right cross.

Covering Up

If you've missed your opportunity to slip, block, or parry a punch, or you simply got caught off guard, covering up is your next best option. Once again, this technique will not work as well as it does in boxing. If your opponent is throwing a flurry of punches, you will only be able to cover up for so long before one of his punches slips past your arms and connects with your face. In order to prevent this from happening, you must retaliate with strikes of your own, go for a takedown, or move out of the way. And the only way you can exercise any of these options is to maintain a proper fighting stance while covering up. Although it is difficult, you mustn't lean too far back, cross your feet, or spread your legs out wide. If you keep your cool and take advantage of openings as soon as you see them, you'll have a much better chance of survival.

 I'm in a fighting stance, looking for an opening.

2 Jason advances with a flurry of punches, catching me off guard. Tucking my chin and keeping my eyes on Jason's chest, I raise both arms to protect my face. It is important to remember that this is a temporary position. The longer you stay here, the greater chance you'll have of getting knocked out. Keep your eyes on your opponent, and when you see an opening, take it.

Faking a Shoot to the Right Cross

This is a great move to use on an opponent who keeps dropping his hands every time you go to shoot. If you land the cross, there is a good chance that you'll knock your opponent out. And if you land the cross but don't knock your opponent out, your opponent will most likely be more hesitant to drop his hands the next time you shoot, which will make easier it to get the takedown.

1 I'm in a fighting stance, looking for an opening.

2 I drop down into a low sprinter's stance like I'm going to shoot in for Jason's legs. Jason drops his hands to defend against my shoot.

3 Instead of shooting in for the takedown, I snap my hips in a counterclockwise direction and throw a right cross to Jason's jaw.

Faking a Shoot to the Uppercut

Sometimes faking the shoot and throwing the cross doesn't work because your opponent keeps his arms up to protect his face. But just because your opponent's arms are up doesn't necessarily mean that you can't hit him in the face. If he's leaving a gap between his arms, targeting his chin with an uppercut is a great option.

1 I'm in a fighting stance, looking for an opening.

2 I drop down into a low sprinter's stance like I'm going to shoot in for Jason's legs. Fearful that I'm going to throw a right cross, Jason keeps his arms up to shield his face.

3 Snapping my hips in a counterclockwise direction, I sneak an uppercut between his elbows and strike his chin. It is important not to drop your hand down to gather power for your uppercut because this will not only take power away from your punch, but also telegraph your intentions. If your opponent pinches his arms closer together in anticipation, you run the risk of punching his elbow and breaking your hand.

Faking a Shoot to the Hook

If you fake a shoot and nail your opponent with a good uppercut, the chances are the next time you fake a shoot and he decides to cover up, his elbows will be pinched tightly together. This will make it hard to land a cross or an upper-cut, but it sets you up nicely to snap a hook around his block-ade and strike either his neck or the side of his jaw.

1 I'm in a fighting stance, looking for an opening.

2 I drop down into a low sprinter's stance like I'm going to shoot in for Jason's legs. Fearful that I'm going to throw either a right cross or an uppercut, Jason keeps his arms up and his elbows pinched together to shield his face.

3 Taking a small step to my left with my lead leg, I turn my hips and shoulders in a counterclockwise direction and slightly bend my knees.

4 I lift my left elbow so that it's level with my shoulder. Keeping my arm bent at a forty-five-degree angle, I snap my hips in a clockwise direction and throw a hook into the right side of Jason's chin.

Countering a Roundhouse Kick with a Cross

If your opponent throws a roundhouse kick, the right cross can be an excellent counter. In order for this technique to work, however, you must land the right cross before your opponent lands the kick. If your opponent has a fast kick, then you're going to have to be able to read his movements and see the kick coming before his foot lifts off the ground. If he is lazy with his kicks, you're going to have a little more time, but you still must have good timing. The last thing you want is to distribute additional weight over your lead leg for the punch and then get struck full force with a roundhouse kick to your thigh. If you are uncertain how to spot a kick coming, then it's best just to check your opponent's kick, which we will describe how to do shortly.

1 I'm in a fighting stance, eyes trained on the center of Jason's chest to monitor his movement and anticipate his next attack.

2 I see Jason take a small step forward with his left leg and begin turning his hips in a counterclockwise direction, notifying me that he's about to throw a roundhouse kick. Immediately I snap my hips in a counterclockwise direction and throw a cross straight into Jason's jaw. Because my attack is linear and Jason's attack is circular, my attack lands first, knocking him off balance and taking the sting out of his kick.

■ Kicking

The ability to kick your opponent in the head or leg is a true asset in every fight, but not all kicks are created equal. Flashy karate kicks such as the crescent kick or the axe kick usually do not work in MMA competition. By utilizing them, you will only open yourself up for a takedown or a stern right hand. In MMA competition, you generally want to use a few basic kicks that have been proven time and again at the top levels of competition. These kicks have ended many fights, but if you do not know how to execute them properly, it is better not to attempt them. Seldom do you see a striker who has never before grappled try to take his opponent to the ground and lock in a submission hold, and it should work the other way around. If you plan on kicking during a fight, master it before you do. Spend time breaking it down, learning all of its nuances, and then test it out while sparring. If you try a kick for the first time in actual combat, there is a high probability that you're going to get knocked out.

Round Kick

If you plan on learning only one kick, make it the roundhouse kick. It is a monster of a kick, capable of ending a fight in a split second if done right. It is, however, not an easy kick to learn, and if you want to use it effectively in competition, it has to be done right.

So before we get into the *when* and *where*, let's talk a little bit about the *how*. From your normal fighting stance, you are going to take a step with your lead leg. The distance of that step all depends upon where you are in relation to your opponent. If your opponent is outside of range, you want to take

a fairly large step. If your opponent is within range, that step might just be a few inches. Once you get really good at this kick, you'll even be able to take a small step backward if your opponent is too close. In any fashion, you want to take a step with that lead leg. Next, you are going to push off the ball of your rear foot so that your hips spin in the direction that you are kicking. It is important that your hips spin in a circle rather than forward because nothing about this kick is linear. If you get your foot or hip moving forward, you are going to lose a tremendous amount of power.

Once you get your hips in motion, you are going to want to forget about your rear leg, which is going to be your kicking leg. Just forget about it, it's not important at this point. If you dwell or focus on your rear leg or the kick, it's going to come out like a karate kick. And if it comes out like a karate kick, there is no point in throwing it. So just focus on your hips. As they start to spin, they're going to rotate your entire body on the ball of your lead foot. By the time your hips and the toes of your lead foot are facing the complete opposite direction of your opponent, your rear leg will automatically get pulled off the ground. You've just sent your hips in a near circle, and now your rear leg wants to catch up, so let it. Stay relaxed, let you leg whip around in a circle all on it's own. You don't need to add any muscle; you've just got to steer your shin toward its target. I said "shin" rather than "foot" because that's the part of your leg that's going to make contact with your opponent. If you do a proper roundhouse kick and make contact with your foot, the chances are you'll break half a dozen very small bones.

It's a difficult kick to master, but if you practice it on a punching bag in front of the mirror there are several things you can look for to see if you're doing it right. The first thing you should look at is your lead foot. If the heel of your lead foot is not pointed at your opponent when your kick makes contract, you're going to need to go back to the drawing board and work on spinning. Although it seems rather silly, it helps to think of yourself as a ballerina, pushing off your rear leg so you spin around and around on the ball of your lead foot. Once you have that down, keep the spin exactly how it was, only now guide your rear leg off the ground so that your shin makes contact with the punching bag.

After you get your lead heel facing your opponent at the point of contact, watch your head in the mirror when you throw the kick. It should remain in the same position from the beginning of the kick to the end. If it moves up or down, it means that you are jumping into the kick. If you head moves forward, it means that you are leaning into the kick rather than spinning. If your head moves from side to side, it either means you are trying to kick too high or you are trying to muscle the kick. It can also mean that you are simply getting off balance. If this is the case, you can throw your rear arm down to your side just as the kick comes off the ground. This will not only give you more balance, but also help you spin and generate more power. It is important that you get all these little subtleties right *before* you use the kick in competition. If your kick isn't up to par, you will not only be doing little to no damage to your opponent, but you will also be setting your opponent up for a hard cross or a takedown.

Now that we've thoroughly covered the *how* part of the kick, let's focus on the *where*. Generally in MMA competition you want to throw the roundhouse kick to your opponent's lead thigh, really dig it into the soft tissue above his knee. This will slowly chop your opponent down, and many, many fights have been won this way. Some of those fights were won because the person absorbing the kicks gave up due to the pain, and other fights were won because the person absorbing all the kicks dropped his hands to block the kick and opened himself up for a hard cross. Now if your opponent is off balance, dazed from a previous shot, or simply gassed out from a long and hard battle, you can target the roundhouse kick up high. You can aim at the side of your opponent's head, but that is not the choice location. If you have the flexibility, you want to cast the kick over your opponent's shoulder and then angle it down to the side of his neck and jaw. This will not only be easier on your shinbone, but also cause much more damage to your opponent. The other prime target for the roundhouse kick is to your opponent's liver or ribs, but you have to be really selective with these shots because there is always the chance that your opponent will snatch your kick and then take you down. If you have a solid roundhouse kick, he will not be able to do this without causing himself some damage, but if you're looking to keep the fight standing, targeting your opponent's leg is a much better option.

The last thing we need to cover is *when*. If you can lash your leg out and then regain your fighting stance as quickly as the pros in Thailand, then pretty much anytime is a good time. If your kick is good but not that good, you'll usually want to set it up first, and for the rear roundhouse kick the best set up is the jab. When you throw a proper jab, your hips are going to spin slightly in a clockwise direction as the punch goes out. As you pull your punch back, your hips are going to return to your fighting stance by spinning in a counterclockwise direction. Your rear roundhouse kick is fueled by a counterclockwise spin of your hips, so just keep that spin going past your regular fighting stance, straight into the kick. It's perfect timing because you've already set it up with the jab. Then the only thing you need to watch out for, really watch out for, is your opponent countering with a cross. The cross is the archrival of the roundhouse kick.

1 From my fighting stance, I see an opening to throw a roundhouse kick to Jason's lead leg.

2 After taking a small step forward with my left foot, I push off the ground with my right foot to get my hips spinning in a counterclockwise direction. The motion that I have created, which is circular rather than linear, forces my lower body to pivot on the ball of my left foot. This automatically pulls my right foot off the ground, and I let it whip around so that my shin clashes into Jason's thigh just above the knee. It is important to note that this is not a kick you should muscle. Keep your leg relaxed and don't think about how you are going to retract your leg before it lands. If you stay relaxed and keep your upper body erect, the impact of the kick will send your leg back to your fighting stance naturally.

Inside Leg Kick

In many ways, the inside leg kick is like a jab. The kick most likely isn't going to cause your opponent any major damage, but you can use it to unbalance your opponent, set up another strike, or simply wear your opponent down over time. If you are able to land ten or twenty inside leg kicks over the course of a single round, you're going to take considerable sting off your opponent's speed and power in virtually all aspects of his game.

1 I'm in a fighting stance with Jason circling around me in a counter-clockwise direction.

2 As Jason plants his weight on his lead leg, I take a small step with my right foot.

3 Immediately after stepping with my right foot, I jerk my hips in a clockwise direction and spin on the ball of my right foot. This whips my left shin up into the soft tissue of Jason's inner thigh, just below his groin. It is important to note that when doing this kick, the less movement that you have with your upper body the better. If your head bobs up or down or you move from side to side, your opponent will see the kick coming and either lift his front leg to check it or retaliate with a punch.

Front Kick

The front kick is not a heavily utilized kick in MMA competition, but it does have its time and place. It is best used to keep your opponent from rapidly advancing, but your timing has to be precise in order to be successful with it. If you throw the kick too early, you are not only going to miss your target, but you're also going to be out of your fighting stance when your opponent rushes in. If you throw it too late, your opponent is going to squash your kick before you can lash your foot out, throwing you off balance and making you susceptible to a takedown or strikes. The kick can also be used on a stationary opponent to set up both a takedown and a number of strikes. To bring your opponent's head and arms down to land punches, you want to target his lead hip. If you want to take the breath out of your opponent and unbalance him for a takedown, you can target his sternum. But no matter where you are targeting the kick, it is important never to get overextended. If you get overextended, you're going to be vulnerable. To keep this from happening, practice throwing the kick into open air. You want to be able to throw it out and back without falling forward. That way, when you throw the kick in competition and your foot either slips off your opponent's body or you just plain miss, you won't fall into your opponent's punches.

1 While searching for an opening, I can tell by Jason's movements that he's going to advance with a string of punches. To fend him off, I prepare to throw a front kick to his hip.

2 Redistributing the majority of my weight to my right leg, I snap my left knee up to my chest. I thrust the ball of my left foot into Jason's hip, leaning back slightly to maintain my balance. It is important to note that after the kick has landed, you do not want to let your kicking leg drop straight to the floor. You want to bring it back while it's still in the air and then return immediately to your fighting stance.

Checking

If you've ever been hit in the leg, ribs, or head with a hard roundhouse kick, then you know the importance of learning how to check. If you haven't felt what it's like to absorb the brunt of one of these blows, take it from me—it hurts. A strong roundhouse kick can break a neck, shatter ribs, or tear so deep into the thigh muscle that standing is no longer an option. With more and more MMA competitors learning how to throw the roundhouse kick properly, checking has become a mandatory tool for survival. It's still going to hurt, but if you do it properly, raising your leg on the side of your body that the kick is attacking and blocking the kick with your shin, the chances are it'll hurt your opponent much worse that it hurts you.

The difficult part of checking is getting a handle on both the technique and timing. Technique can be improved by doing hundreds and hundreds of mock checks in the mirror, correcting your mistakes the moment you notice them. To give you an idea of what the correct movement should be, let's take you through the check. If your opponent throws a rear roundhouse kick to your lead leg, which is the most popular destination, you want to lean back slightly so the majority of your weight is over your rear leg. Keeping your rear butt cheek clenched tight and your groin thrust slightly forward, you want to raise your lead leg. If you imagine there's a big circle around you, and your opponent is standing at twelve o'clock, then you raise your leg so that your knee is pointing directly at nine o'clock. Because it can sometimes be hard to tell exactly where your opponent's kick is headed, you also want to rotate your upper body just

enough so that you can place the bottom of your lead elbow just on the outside of your rising knee. This will create a shield on that whole side of your body. It is important that you make that slight rotation with your upper body so that you're not letting your lead arm stray too far from your side when you place it on the outside of your knee. The strong roundhouse kick can easily break bones, so if it hits your arm, you are going to need your body to absorb some of the blow.

When the kick collides with your shin, you're going to want to be standing erect with your hips thrust forward and your rear butt cheek tight. If you are not standing erect or keeping your groin forward, the kick will most likely drive through your shin and crash into your rear leg, sweeping you off your feet. It is important that you stand your ground and not be afraid. You don't want to make your lead leg rigid, but you don't want it to be completely relaxed either.

Timing is a little more difficult to get the hang of, and it can only be obtained by doing hours upon hours of checking drills with your training partner. To do this drill, you are both going to want to wear shin pads. Don't try to straighten your shins by doing checking drills without pads because it will have the opposite effect. The best Muay Thai kickboxers in Thailand use pads when drilling checks, and so should you. So once you both have on the proper gear, square off in your fighting stances. Have your opponent throw a kick to your leg and check it, and then throw a kick to you opponent's leg. Go back and forth until you understand proper technique, and then move on to rib kicks. Once you have become a master at checking rib kicks, start moving around with your opponent and exchanging kicks. Eventually, you'll learn how to spot the roundhouse kick coming and no longer need to go kick for kick. You'll be able to move into what is called leg sparring, throwing the roundhouse kick whenever you see an opening and checking every kick that comes at you.

1 As I twist my hips to throw a kick to Jason's lead leg, he spots my movement. Realizing my kick is aimed at his leg, he lifts his left knee at a forty-five-degree angle to his hips. If my kick were aimed at his ribs, he would twist his upper body slightly in a clockwise direction and place his left arm on the outside of his left knee, shielding the entire left side of his body. With both checks, he is going to use his shin to block the kick. It is important to note that immediately after you block the kick you drop your left foot back into your fighting stance. While your opponent recovers from the checked kick, you can immediately launch an attack of your own.

Kicking under the Check

If you throw the roundhouse kick and your opponent checks it with his shin, it's often going to hurt you more than it hurts him. If you've put in your hours kicking the heavy bag and partaking in checking drills, then your shins will most likely be able to handle the punishment, but there is no need to take unnecessary abuse. One option is to set your roundhouse kicks up with punches, and another option is to target your roundhouse kick below your opponent's check. The latter is best to do after throwing several ribs kicks because your opponent will most likely have fallen into a pattern of lifting his lead leg high off the ground. The kick is going to target your opponent's rear calf, and in addition to causing him a great deal of pain, it will also sweep him right off his feet.

1 Jason has checked several of my roundhouse kicks to his ribs, so I decide to change my striking pattern and kick below his check.

2 I take a small step with my left foot, same as I would if I were going to kick Jason in the leg or ribs.

3 As I whip my hips around, Jason anticipates my roundhouse kick and lifts his lead leg to check it. Before my right foot comes off the ground, I bend more prominently on my left leg. This allows me to guide my kick underneath Jason's left foot and strike his right calf with my shin. If this kick is landed with power, you'll most likely kick your opponent's leg right out from under him, and he'll end up on his back.

Knee Strike

The knee is an excellent striking tool that has been used quite effectively in MMA competition. It can be utilized to create distance between you and your opponent when you're covering up from a flurry of punches. It can be used to knock your opponent out when he shoots for a takedown, and it can be used as an offensive strike to finish off a combination.

1 I'm in a fighting stance, looking for an opening.

2 Jason drops down to a sprinter's stance. As he shoots in for a takedown, I place my hands on his head to slow his forward momentum.

3 As Jason propels his body toward my legs, I bring up my right knee into his jaw. It is important to note that if your opponent has kept his hands up, there is still a chance that he'll continue to drive forward for the takedown after you throw the knee. Because of this, you must bring your knee back as quickly as possible so you can sprawl if necessary.

Front Kick Parry to Hook

If your opponent constantly throws front kicks to keep you out of punching range, knowing how to parry his kick is a useful tool. Not only will it throw off your opponent's balance, but it will also set you up nicely to land a solid hook to your opponent's jaw.

1 I'm in a fighting stance, trying to stay within punching range.

2 Jason throws a front kick to keep me at bay.

3 Dropping my right hand, I scoop under Jason's ankle and redirect his kick to the outside of my body.

4 I take a small step with my left foot, slightly turning my hips and shoulders in a counterclockwise direction to build power for the punch.

5 Snapping my hips in a clockwise direction, I throw a hook to Jason's jaw.

■ Combinations

Now that you have some basic strikes in your arsenal, it's time to start putting them together in combinations. The ones I have laid out below will help you get started, but by no means should you stop there. As you begin to spar with your training partner, you'll get a feel for how one strike can set up another. It's important that you take advantage of these setups. Your opponent will have a much easier time defending a single strike than he will a half dozen of them launched in succession, especially if you interchange those strikes between his legs, body, and head. Although it can often be intimidating committing to a string of punches and kicks because you never know how your opponent will retaliate, it's going to be much more intimidating for your opponent. And the more comfortable you get throwing combos, the better you will become at changing your game plan in mid-attack to deal with your opponent's reactions.

Combination One: Jab, Roundhouse Kick

1 I'm in a fighting stance, looking for an opening.

2 I throw a jab at Jason's chin. In addition to wobbling him, it also covers his vision for a split second.

3 As I pull my left shoulder back, I use the momentum to help spin my hips in a counterclockwise direction and launch a roundhouse kick to Jason's thigh with my right leg.

Combination Two: Jab, Cross, Inside Leg Kick

1 I'm in a fighting stance, looking to set up a combination.

2 I throw a jab into Jason's face, blinding him for a split second.

3 As I pull my left shoulder back, I use the momentum to spin my hips in a counterclockwise direction and throw a cross to Jason's face.

4 As I pull my right shoulder back, I use the momentum to spin my hips in a clockwise direction and launch an inside leg kick to the inner thigh of Jason's left leg.

Combination Three: Inside Leg Kick, Cross, Knee

1 I'm in a fighting stance, looking to set up a combination.

2 After taking a small step with my right foot, I throw an inside leg kick to Jason's lead thigh to throw him off balance and get him to drop his hands.

3 As I pull my left leg back, I use the momentum to throw a right cross to Jason's chin.

4 Stunned from the powerful shot, Jason's first reaction is to take me to the ground so he can recover. As he drops low to shoot for my legs, I drop my hands to his head to slow his forward momentum.

5 As Jason drives his body into mine, I lift my right knee to his jaw.

■ Striking from the Clinch

The clinch can either be your best friend or worst enemy. If you've spent little or no time tying up with your training partners while sparring, the clinch will most likely be your worst enemy. Striking from the clinch is not the same as striking at an opponent while moving freely on your feet. I've seen MMA competitors with savage punches and kicks become little more than punching bags in the clinch, and I've seen MMA competitors who couldn't throw a punch or kick if

their life depended upon it suddenly turn into a striking machine the moment they're tied up. The clinch is a different universe entirely. It requires that you learn how to read your opponent's movements by feel rather than sight. It requires different stamina, different balance, different footwork, different stances, different setups, and different strikes. The techniques I have laid out below will get you headed down the right road, but the only way to turn the clinch into your best friend is through hundreds of hours of practice.

The Thai Clinch

1 To achieve this position, clasp your hands together at the base of your opponent's skull and pinch your forearms together around his neck. Place your head slightly to one side of your opponent's head and arch your back to allow room to throw knees.

Collar and Arm Clinch

1 achieve this position wrap one hand around the back of your opponent's neck and hook your other hand over his arm.

Outside Knee

Although most knee strikes are designed to hit your opponent like a spear, this one is not. The outside knee from the clinch position is much like the hook in that it's a circular strike. It's often a hard technique to learn, so practicing the technique on the heavy bag can definitely help. To do this, wrap your arms around the bag and pinch your forearms together as if it were an opponent's neck. Then lift your rear leg on the outside of the bag so that your knee is level with your target. Hold it there for several moments just to make sure that you have no upward momentum. Then, bring your knee from the side into the bag, making contact with the inside of your knee. This technique isn't a knockout shot, but it can definitely steal your opponent's breath, break ribs, and wear him down over time.

1 I've established the Thai clinch position by clasping my hands together at the base of Jason's skull and pinching his neck between my forearms.

2-3 I lift my right knee up on the outside of Jason's body, stopping its ascent when it's on the same plane as Jason's ribs. With a quick snap of my hips, I cast my knee on a horizontal plane into Jason's ribs. It is important to note that this knee strike is circular. Your knee should chop into your opponent's side rather than thrust into it.

Inside Knee

The inside knee is a lot more powerful that the outside knee, and when you land one square on your opponent's sternum, there's a good chance he'll go down. But it can also be a little tricky to learn how to do it right. Most people want to bring their knee straight up to their target. This is fine when you want upward momentum, such as when your opponent drops his head to shoot for your legs, but in order to get the most out of the strike from the clinch position, you're going to want to bring your knee up on the outside of your opponent's body first, just as you did with the outside knee. Once it is on the same level as your target, a quick snap of your hips will pull your knee to the inside of your opponent's body and send it straight into your target. If your target is your opponent's sternum, you won't just graze it as you would with a knee traveling upward, but rather dig deep into it, causing much more damage.

1 I've established the Thai clinch position by clasping my hands together at the base of Jason's skull and pinching his neck between my forearms.

2 Instead of lifting my knee straight up into Jason's chest, I bring it up on the outside of his body.

3 Once my knee is at the same level as Jason's sternum, I snap my hips in a counterclockwise direction and spin slightly on the ball of my left foot. The rotation of my hips not only brings my knee to the inside of our bodies, but also helps to push my knee straight into Jason's sternum.

Inside and Outside Knee to Thigh

When you fight an opponent who has good defense in the clinch, it can be difficult to land powerful shots to his body and head. If this is the case, a good alternative is to attack his legs with your knees. Although these shots won't knock your opponent out, they can certainly be painful and wear him down over time. The more of these little shots that you land, the harder it will be for him to shoot or even throw a punch. If you can successfully take out your opponent's legs, make it so that he has to lock his knees just to stand, usually the knockout isn't far off.

1 I've established the Thai clinch position by clasping my hands together at the base of Jason's skull and pinching his neck between my forearms.

2 I skip my left leg back to set up my first knee strike.

3 To take away Jason's balance, I tug his head down and to the right. As I do this, I shoot my left knee forward into the soft tissue of his inner thigh, just above his knee.

4 I drop back into my fighting stance to set up my next knee strike.

5 I lift my right leg on the outside of Jason's body.

6 Tugging on Jason's head, I drop my right knee into Jason's thigh, just above his knee.

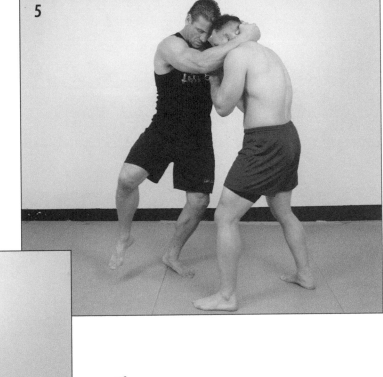

Knee to Head from Clinch

When I fought Kimo Leopoldo in UFC 48, held on June 19, 2004, we tied up in the clinch just a few seconds into the bout. He had put a considerable amount of work into learning how to fight from the ground, and I guess he wanted to test it out on me. His goal was to take me down; I could tell that the moment we tied up, but he didn't go about it in a smart way. He kept dropping his head low, trying to reach down and snatch my legs. The moment he dropped his head too low on the outside of my body, I brought a knee up into his face. It didn't knock him out, but it landed hard enough to get his attention. If my focus had been absorbed by the battle we had going with our arms, I could have easily missed the opportunity to land a good blow. So while it is important to always be on the lookout for uppercuts and hooks while tied up in the clinch, it is also important to remember that your knees are effective weapons, especially when your opponent starts dropping his head.

1 I'm tied up in the clinch with Jason, working to unbalance him so I can go for a strike.

2 As Jason and I pummel, I hook my left arm over his right arm and grab hold of his left biceps.

3 As Jason dips his head down to snatch one of my legs, I lock my left arm tight around his right arm and push his left arm into his body with my right hand. This not only gives me good control of his body, but also creates the space needed to bring my right knee up on the outside of our arms and into his face.

Knee to Head from Clinch (Variation)

1 Pummeling for position in the clinch, I hook my left arm over Jason's right arm and grab his left biceps with my right hand.

2 Tightening my left arm around Jason's right arm, I take a step back with my right leg and turn my body to the side. To keep Jason from turning into me, I push on the right side of his face with my right hand.

3 With Jason's right arm trapped under my left arm, he can't pull away from me. And with my right hand pushing on the right side of his face, he can't turn into me. If he tries dropping low to go for my legs, it's only going to create a greater impact as I bring my right knee up into his face.

Under-Hooks to Knee

As I mentioned earlier, I landed a pretty good knee to Kimo Leopoldo's face while we were tied up in the clinch at UFC 48. It didn't knock him out, but I thought it would be enough to stop him from dropping his head low. I was wrong. A few seconds later, still pummeling in the clinch, I managed to sneak both my arms underneath his arms. From this position, I could clasp my hands together behind Kimo's back and do all sorts of fun stuff. He didn't want to hang around to see what I had in store, so he tried to back out before I could lock my hands together. The only way he could do that, however, was by dropping his head. The moment his head came down, I brought up a power-bomb of a knee that knocked him out cold. I could have worked to keep my under-hooks instead, but it wouldn't have resulted in the same positive outcome. So whether your opponent is pushing into you or trying to escape from the clinch, you should always remember your knees. If your opponent drops his head low, they can be your ticket to the knockout.

1 Pummeling for position in the clinch, I hook my left arm over Jason's right arm and grab his left biceps with my right hand. Pushing on Jason's left arm with my right hand, I create space between our bodies.

2 Using the space that I've created between Jason's body and my body, I slip my right arm underneath his left armpit.

3 Turning my hips in a counterclockwise direction, I create space to slip my left arm underneath Jason's right armpit. Now that I have the double under-hooks, I can clasp my hands together behind Jason's back and pull his hips into me, disrupting his balance and making it easier to get a takedown.

4 Before I can clasp my hands together, Jason tries to back out. I keep upward pressure on his arms to force him to drop his head in order to escape.

5 Without having to worry about Jason grabbing either of my legs, I bring my right knee up to his jaw.

Elbow

A good Muay Thai kickboxer can throw a dozen different elbow strikes from the clinch, all of them effective. They throw elbows over their opponent's guard, from the side, or up to their opponent's chin. The trick to getting the most out of elbow strikes is staying relaxed. Just as with most of the strikes we have covered, you're going to generate power for the blow from your hips. If you stay relaxed and land a good shot with the point of your elbow, you'll most likely open a cut on your opponent's face. If you land a few more, there's a good chance he'll go to sleep.

1 I've established a collar and arm clinch by wrapping my right hand around the back of Jason's neck and controlling his right arm with my left hand.

2 Wrapping my left hand behind Jason's neck, I hook his left arm with my right hand and throw it to the outside.

3 With Jason's left arm out of the way, I snap my right elbow into his jaw.

Uppercut

Unlike the jab or cross, the uppercut works best when you're in tight with your opponent. It's not a powerhouse of a strike, but since its target is the sweet spot on your opponent's chin, it can easily render a knockout. As with all strikes, the trick to getting the most bang for your buck is to relax, use your hips, and not add any additional muscle.

1 I've established a collar and arm clinch by wrapping my left hand around the back of Jason's neck and controlling his left arm with my right hand.

2 I drop my right hand just below Jason's left arm.

3 Still controlling Jason's head with my left hand, I bend my knees slightly and position my right fist so that my palm is facing my chest. Then, with a quick counterclockwise snap of my hips, I thrust my right fist up into Jason's jaw. It is important to note that, as with most strikes, the power behind the uppercut is largely generated from your hips, so there is no need to dramatically dip your hand.

Upward Elbow from Clinch

Raising an elbow up into your opponent's jaw can be a great substitute for the uppercut because it's not only a harder strike, but it also eliminates the possibility of breaking your hand.

1 I've established a collar and arm clinch by wrapping my left hand around the back of Jason's neck and controlling his left arm with my right hand.

2 I slip my right hand underneath Jason's left arm.

3 Snapping my hips in a counterclockwise direction, I thrust my right elbow up into Jason's jaw.

13

Takedowns

IF A COMPETITOR CAN LAND PUNCHES AND KICKS while on his feet and lock in submission holds while on the ground, he can consider himself a competent fighter. In order to be a complete fighter, however, a competitor must also be able to transition back and forth between the standing and ground phases of combat. The first half of such a skill, bringing the fight from the feet to the ground, is not easy to master. With virtually every MMA competitor having learned how to defend against the most common takedowns, persistence isn't always the answer. If you attempt numerous single-leg takedowns in a row, your opponent will dial in your movement. He'll know what to expect, making it easier for him to build a strong defense. But if you attempt a number of single-leg takedowns and then switch to another technique, such as a takedown from the clinch, you'll keep your opponent guessing and possibly catch him off guard. This is why I have shared several different takedowns in the following pages that have the same end. You might find that you are better at certain takedowns than others, but it's important to pack as many takedown techniques into your arsenal as possible so you don't get stuck in the standing phase of combat. It doesn't matter how hard you can punch and kick; there will always be someone who can punch and kick harder. In order to dominate a fight, any fight, you must have the ability to dictate where

the fight will transpire. If you rely on a single takedown or your attempts to bring the fight to the ground are weak and sloppy, half your game can fly right out the window.

■ Shooting for the Takedown

The shoot is an explosive movement where you drop down into a low sprinter's stance and then launch your body into your opponent's legs for a takedown. If you watch an MMA competition, you can immediately tell who has worked on developing a mean shoot and who hasn't. The competitor with a mean shoot doesn't blindly charge in for his opponent's legs. He waits for an opportune moment, such as when his opponent is off balance or crossing his feet. And if his opponent's balance is keen, he sets his shoot up with punches or baits his opponent to punch. Then he drops down really low, keeps his hands up to protect his face, and drives his body straight through his opponent's legs.

It definitely takes some work to develop a mean shoot, but since it will most likely be your primary method of bringing a fight to the ground, it's definitely worth spending some time on. If you are new to the shoot, I recommend that you start by shooting in for the single- and double-leg takedown from within striking distance. Once you are able to haul your opponent to the ground time and again at close range, start practicing your shoot from outside striking distance. After you've had some success there, move on to the more advanced techniques such as the sunset flip. By the time you get a handle on that, you'll be ready to shoot in on your opponent, get the takedown, and then transition directly into a submission hold. As with all techniques in submission fighting, practice makes perfect. If you plan on training three times a week, then at least fifteen minutes from each session should be delegated to working exclusively on your shoot.

Single-Leg Takedown off a Punch

If you can execute a single-leg takedown with proper timing and speed, the technique is virtually irreplaceable. But despite its effectiveness, randomly shooting for your opponent's legs and hoping for the best usually won't work. If your opponent sees your shoot coming, he will most likely sprawl back his hips and legs and drive his weight down on top of you, leaving you in a very vulnerable position. To increase your chances of penetrating your opponent's legs, you want to set your shoot up, and waiting for your opponent to punch is as good a setup as any. The moment your opponent lashes out with his fist, he's going to be exposed. His primary focus will be landing the punch, and with a larger percentage of his weight distributed on either his front or rear leg, his ability to effectively sprawl will be greatly reduced. The key to making this technique a success is timing, and the only way to develop good timing is to spend countless hours in the gym sparring. You need to learn how to see a punch coming. If you shoot in too early, your opponent will abandon his punch and sprawl. If you wait too long, you're probably going to eat a shot.

1 I work into striking range, baiting Jason to throw a punch.

2 I watch Jason's center and monitor his movements. His hips suddenly snap in a counterclockwise direction and a large percentage of his weight is distributed to his lead leg, telling me that he's about to throw a right cross. Just as his fist lashes out, I drop underneath the punch into a low sprinter's stance. With the majority of my weight over my lead leg, I start driving forward off my left foot. It is important to note that I have kept my hands up to protect my face from a knee or kick.

3 I drive hard off my left foot and shoot my body into Jason's lead leg. With my head on the inside of Jason's left leg, I scoop his calf with my right arm and grab his ankle with my left hand. It is important to note that I have shot my body to the outside of Jason's lead leg. This will not only help with the takedown, but also make it harder for Jason to strike at my face.

4 As I stand up, I pull Jason's ankle toward the ceiling with my left hand while driving my shoulders down into his knee and thigh.

5 Forcing Jason to the ground, I maintain control of his left leg to hinder him from climbing back to his feet or scrambling on the ground.

6 Moving my body to the outside Jason's left leg, I come down on top of him and assume the side mount position.

Ankle Pick

The ankle pick is a single-leg takedown used quite often in MMA competition because it reduces your opponent's ability to strike your face with his hands. When practicing this move in training, make sure your sparring partner doesn't lock his lead leg straight while in his fighting stance. If he does, there's a good chance he'll end up with a broken leg.

1 I work into striking range, baiting Jason to throw a punch.

2 I watch Jason's center and monitor his movements. His hips suddenly snap in a counterclockwise direction and a large percentage of his weight is distributed to his lead leg, telling me that he's about to throw a right cross. Just as his fist lashes out, I drop underneath the punch into a low sprinter's stance. With the majority of my weight over my lead leg, I start driving forward off my left foot. In order to protect my face from either a knee or kick, I have kept my hands up.

3 As I drive my weight forward, I shoot my head to the outside of Jason's left leg and wrap my left hand around the inside of Jason's left ankle and my right forearm around the outside of his ankle. Pulling Jason's left ankle toward my chest with my arms, I drive my left shoulder into his thigh just above his knee. It is important to note that the lower you drive your shoulder into your opponent's leg, the easier it will be to take him down.

4 As Jason falls to his back, I maintain control of his left leg so I can safely work my body around to his left side and obtain a side mount position.

Double-Leg Takedown

This is a double-leg takedown where your head is going to come into play. Instead of driving your head to the side of your opponent's body, you're going to drive it directly into your opponent's midsection like a spear. Before executing this technique with full force, you should practice it in slow motion several times. This will help you get a feel for the proper movement so you don't injure your neck.

1 I work into striking range, baiting Jason to throw a punch so I can set up a takedown

2 Watching Jason's center and monitoring his movements, I see him snap his hips in a counterclockwise direction, telling me that he is about to throw a right cross. Just as his fist lashes out, I drop underneath the punch into a low sprinter's stance. With the majority of my weight over my lead leg, I start driving forward. In order to protect my face from either a knee or kick, I keep my hands up.

3 Instead of driving my head to the outside of Jason's body, I drive it directly into his midsection. As I do this, I wrap my left hand around Jason's right hamstring and my right hand around Jason's left hamstring. It is important to note that to increase your chances of a successful takedown, you want to wrap your hands as low as you can on your opponent's legs. The higher up you grab, the easier it will be for your opponent to kick back his legs and sprawl.

4 As Jason gets knocked to his back, I wrap my right arm around his left leg and gain control of his right leg with my left hand.

5 Scooping my left arm underneath Jason's left leg to hinder him from pulling me between his legs and into his guard position, I work my body around to Jason's left side.

6 Dropping my weight down on top of Jason, I achieve a side mount position.

Double-Leg Takedown (Variation)

This is another version of the double-leg takedown. With this technique your goal is to wrap your opponent's legs up tight between your arms. If you can cinch your opponent's legs together, narrowing his base and eliminating his ability to sprawl, you will not only have an easier time toppling him to his back, but you will also have the option of lifting your opponent off the ground, turning him in midair, and then dumping him on his head. It can be a great way to end a fight, as several of today's top MMA competitors have proven.

1 I work into striking range, baiting Jason to throw a punch so I can set up a takedown.

2 Watching Jason's center and monitoring his movements, I see him snap his hips in a counterclockwise direction and distribute a larger percentage of weight to his lead leg, indicating that he is about to throw a right cross. Just as his fist lashes out, I drop underneath the punch into a low sprinter's stance. With the majority of my weight over my lead leg, I start driving forward. In order to protect my face from either a knee or kick, I keep my hands up.

3 Driving my head to the outside of Jason's body, I shoot my left leg between his legs and wrap my hands around his back.

4 Pinching my forearms together and pulling Jason's hips into my body, I step my right foot behind Jason's left leg.

5 As I continue to drive my weight forward, Jason topples to his back. From here I can transition into a side mount position, but instead I keep my right foot hooked underneath Jason's left leg and go for a submission.

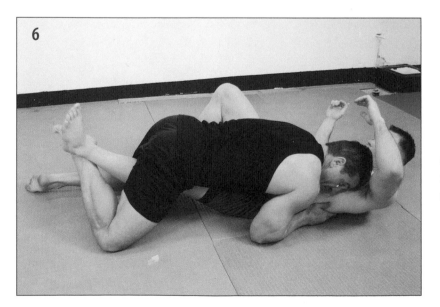

6 With my hips pressing down on Jason's left knee, I pull up on his left ankle with my right foot, causing Jason's left leg to hyperextend.

Sunset Flip to Hammer Lock

When I stepped into the Octagon with Dan Severn, a world-renowned amateur wrestler, in UFC 6, I knew that he was going to shoot for my legs and try to put me on my back. That was his game, grounding his opponents and then pounding on them. So when he dropped for my legs a few minutes into our bout, I sprawled my feet back, wrapped an arm around his head and throat, and sunk in a guillotine choke that forced him to tap in submission. Since that day, a lot of competitors have adopted the guillotine choke, and it has made shooting in on your opponent even more dangerous. If you get caught in this choke while shooting in, the sunset flip is a great technique to employ because it allows you to escape the chokehold and still get the takedown.

1 I've assumed a fighter's stance just outside of striking distance, looking for an opportunity to shoot in on Jason's legs.

2 I drop down to my sprinter's stance, keeping my hands up to avoid catching a knee or kick to the face.

3 As I reach my arms around Jason's legs for a double-leg takedown, he wraps his left arm around my neck and locks in a guillotine choke.

4 I scoot my hips close to Jason's body to increase my leverage. Then I grab around both of his legs and lift him straight off the ground. With Jason's torso resting on my shoulder, I drop into a backward arch.

5-6 When we land, Jason still has the guillotine choke locked in. Pinching his legs together with my arms, I kick my legs over my body.

7-8 Because I have kept Jason's legs pinched together with my arms, he cannot spread his legs and capture me in his guard position. This allows me to step my body to his right side, the opposite side of the choke.

9 Once I assume the side mount position, I grab Jason's left wrist with my right hand and peel it off my head.

10 Trapping Jason's left wrist to the ground with my right hand, I slide my left arm underneath his left triceps muscle.

11 I grab my right wrist with my left hand, creating a figure-four position on Jason's left arm with both of my arms.

12 After planting my left foot behind Jason's head, I push off with my left foot to lift Jason's upper body off the ground. I then push on Jason's left wrist with my right hand while pulling up on his left shoulder with my left arm. This puts a tremendous amount of pressure on Jason's shoulder and elbow.

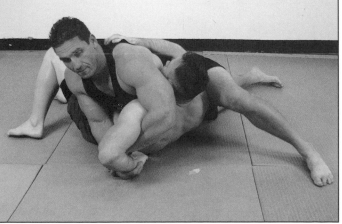

Takedown off Kick to Heel Hook

When fighting an opponent with strong kicks, you to want to be very selective with this technique. If your opponent targets your ribs with a rear roundhouse kick, you should either check the kick with your shin or counter with a strong right cross. The damage you'll receive trying to catch it isn't worth getting the takedown. But when your opponent targets your ribs with a front roundhouse kick, that's a different matter. Unless your opponent skips his front foot back to generate power, the kick isn't going to be as swift or hard, allowing you to catch it without causing yourself serious damage. Before you try this move, however, you first need to learn how to read where your opponent's kick is headed. You can't assume that your opponent will throw a kick to

your ribs because in this day and age competitors are constantly changing their striking patterns. They might go for a rib kick a couple of times, and then throw one to the head. Making assumptions is a good way to get knocked out. So you need to know where your opponent's front foot is headed the moment it comes off the ground. If the kick is aimed at your ribs, you can catch it. If it is aimed at your head, you can duck underneath it and go for the takedown. It is important that you drill these scenarios over and over because if you have to take a second to think about what to do while in a fight, it'll be too late.

1 I've assumed a fighting stance just outside of striking distance, watching Jason's movements and searching for an opportunity to shoot in.

2 Jason targets my ribs with a front roundhouse kick. Just as his kick lands, I wrap my right arm around his calf to keep his leg from bouncing off my ribs.

3 Keeping Jason's left leg trapped tight against my body with my right hand, I push on his shoulder with my opposite hand. It is important to note that many competitors have keen balance while on one foot. If you have trouble shoving your opponent to the ground, lift his trapped leg high into the air to disrupt his balance.

4 As Jason falls to his back, I maintain control of his left leg and step my left foot between his legs.

5 Bending at the knees, I pull Jason's left foot up into my armpit with my right hand.

6   I trap Jason's left leg between my legs and keep his body pinned to the ground by throwing my heels on top of his hips. Then I trap the toes of his left foot under my armpit and hook my right forearm underneath his left heel.

7   Clasping my hands together, I pull up on Jason's left heel with my right forearm while arching my back and pressing my heels down into his hips.

■ Takedowns from the Clinch

The clinch is a great position from which to take your opponent down, as you will see in the upcoming techniques, but nothing in the clinch comes easy. If your opponent is a good Muay Thai kickboxer, he will fight to clasp his hands behind your head so he can drop savage knees to your ribs and sternum. If your opponent is a Greco-Roman wrestler, he'll try fighting for a number of things, including your back. If he gets it, there's a good chance you'll get hefted off your feet and come crashing down on your head. In order to be proficient at taking your opponent down from the clinch, you must first learn how to defend against your opponent's attacks. You must learn how to read and react to his movements. The only way to accomplish this is to spend long hours tied up with your training partners during practice, learning the fundamentals and building the strength needed to pummel for position.

Drop-In Arm Bar

This is a move from the clinch position that works best when your opponent pushes his weight into you. Using your opponent's forward momentum allows you to drop directly into an arm bar and end the fight, but you have to be careful. If your opponent manages to pull his arm free before you can lock in the hold, you'll be left lying on your back with your opponent hovering above you. When you find yourself in this predicament, immediately assume the bottom guard position, which is described in the last section of this book.

1 I've assumed my clinch position by wrapping my right hand tightly around the back of Jason's neck and clinging to Jason's right arm with my left hand.

2 With Jason still tied up in my arms, I take a small step with my right leg toward Jason's right side.

3 I sit down, forcing Jason's body to come with me by pulling on the back of his head with my right arm and his right arm with my left hand.

4 Still pulling down on the back of Jason's head with my right hand, I slide my left arm down Jason's right forearm and trap it to my chest. As I do this, I begin to throw my left leg over to the left side of Jason's head.

5 As I wrap my left leg around Jason's head, I bring my right knee inside his body. It is important to note that while doing this you need to maintain control of your opponent's arm trapped to your chest.

6 Once I force Jason to the ground by pushing with my left leg, I squeeze my knees together to trap his right arm. Gripping his wrist with both hands, I thrust my hips up into Jason's elbow and pull his wrist toward my chest, securing the arm bar.

Figure-Four Throw

When performing the figure-four throw, it is important to stay as tight to your opponent as possible. If your opponent starts pulling his arm free, tie back up in the clinch and search for another option. Getting the takedown from the clinch requires patience. Sometimes you'll have to pummel for five or ten minutes before you can create an opening.

1 Jason and I are tied up in the clinch. To set up the takedown, I wrap my left arm tightly around Jason's right arm.

2 With my right hand, I let go of Jason's left biceps and post it on his chest. As I do this, I grab my right forearm with my left hand, creating a figure-four lock. Once again, I have used both of my arms to bully up on one of Jason's arms.

3-6 I step forward so that Jason and I are body to body, I drop back and spin my body in a counterclockwise direction. To ensure that Jason's body gets whipped over me, I have kept his right arm locked tight in the figure four and my right hand posted on his chest.

7 As Jason gets thrown over to his back, I keep his right arm locked in the figure four until I can roll my body over on top of him.

8 Assuming the side mount position, I release the figure-four lock I had on Jason's right arm and begin hunting for submissions.

Leg Scissor to Knee Bar

When you go for the leg scissor, be sure to commit to it. If you don't commit, then there's a good chance that you'll end up on the ground alone, trying to scramble away from a barrage of downward punches.

1 I'm tied up with Jason in the clinch, pummeling for position. To set up the leg scissor, I hook my left arm tightly over Jason's right arm.

2-3 With my left arm wrapped tightly around Jason's right arm, I leap into him, throwing my left leg across the front of his hips and my right leg behind his legs. As I make a scissor motion with my legs, pushing with my left leg while pulling with my right leg, Jason loses balance and topples to his back.

4 As I hook my right hand around Jason's right leg and pull it toward my body, I pinch my knees together and place my feet on the inside of his left thigh.

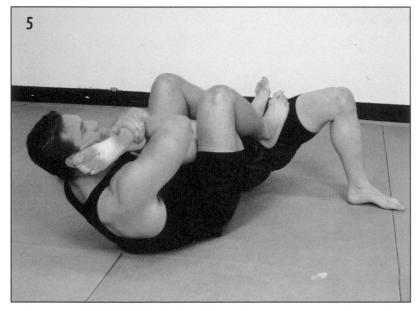

5 To lock in the knee bar, I force Jason's right foot to the right side of my face using my arms and thrust my hips up into his knee.

Hopping Leg Scissor to Heel Hook

A lot of MMA competitors don't perform this takedown because they either don't know it or feel it's too risky. In my opinion, it's a great takedown from the clinch. When I fought Don Frye in the Pride Fighting Championships, he caught me with a punch that nearly sunk my ship. Working on autopilot, I tied up with him in the clinch. As my mind started to clear, I realized that I had performed a flawless hopping leg scissor takedown and fallen directly into a heel hook. If you practice this maneuver enough in training, it becomes second nature. It just requires a little momentum and a lot of technique.

1 I'm pummeling in the clinch with Jason, looking for a takedown.

2 Keeping my left hand cupped around the back of Jason's neck, I throw my left leg over his left hip.

3 I throw my right leg underneath Jason's left hamstring, just above his knee. Pushing down with my left leg and pulling up with my right leg disrupts Jason's balance and topples him to his back.

4 As Jason tries to sit up so he can climb on top of me, I straighten out my legs to force him to his back.

5 Placing my heels on Jason's hips to hold him down, I trap the toes of his left foot underneath my armpit and hook my right forearm underneath his heel.

6-7 Clasping my hands together, I pull up on Jason's left heel with my right forearm while arching my back and pressing my heels down into his hips.

Rolling Knee Bar

If your opponent slips underneath one of your arms and takes your back, as many MMA competitors will do while tied up in the clinch, there are several ways that you can escape the vulnerable position. Tucking and rolling, however, will probably be the one your opponent will least expect.

1 While pummeling in the clinch with Jason, I wrap my left arm tightly over his right arm and grab his left biceps with my right hand.

2 Reaching his left arm across my hips and his right arm behind my back, Jason steps his right leg behind me in an attempt to take my back.

3-4 With my left arm still tightly wrapped over Jason's right arm, I lift my left leg up between his legs and drop to my right shoulder to roll. As I execute the roll, I hook my right arm underneath Jason's right leg.

5 When Jason and I land on our backs, I place my feet on the inside of his left thigh and hook my right arm deeper around his right leg.

6 To lock in the knee bar, I thrust my hips up into Jason's right knee and pull his right foot down to the side of my head with my arms.

■ Wall Takedowns

Turning Opponent for Double-Leg Wall Takedown

Fighting in a cage like the one they have at the Ultimate Fighting Championship is different than fighting in a regular boxing ring. If the fight goes to the clinch and your competitor manages to run you up against the fence, your movement will be limited, making it difficult to land effective strikes or execute a takedown. There are several different ways to escape from this position, but perhaps the best way is to turn your opponent so that his back is pressed up against the fence. Once you achieve this, you'll be in a good position to take your opponent down and then open up with punches. This is the strategy of many top-level MMA competitors, and countless fights have been won in this manner.

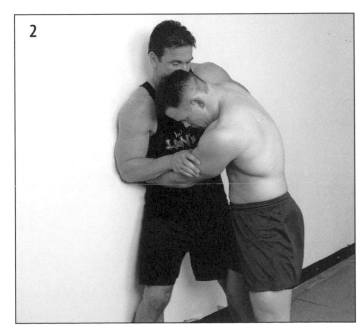

1 While pummeling with Jason in the clinch, I wrap my left arm tightly around his right arm and grab on to his biceps with my right hand.

2 Pushing his weight into me, Jason drives me up against the wall and straightens my body out. It is now difficult for me to turn from side to side or drop low for Jason's legs.

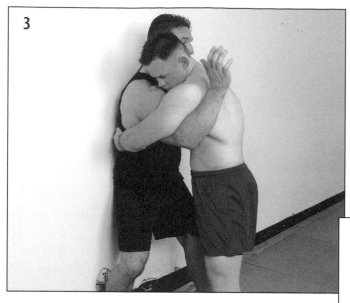

3 Pushing on Jason's left biceps with my right hand, I create enough space to slip my right arm underneath his left armpit.

4 Turning my hips in a counterclockwise direction, I swim my right arm toward the wall while tugging on Jason's right arm with my left arm.

5 As Jason's body is turned against the wall, I drive my weight into him to straighten out his body and limit his mobility.

6 Driving my right shoulder into Jason's body, I turn my left hip out just enough to grab his right biceps with my left hand.

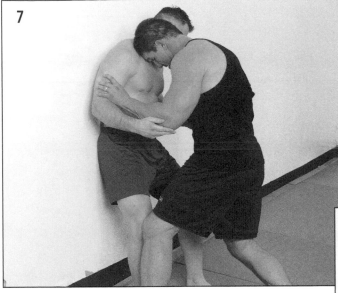

7 Keeping Jason pinned against the wall with my left hand, I grab his left biceps with my right hand.

8 As I keep Jason pinned to the wall with my hands, I drop my head down and drive it into his sternum. Once the pressure from my head keeps Jason pinned against the wall, I let go of his biceps and scoop my left hand around his right leg and my right hand around his left leg.

9 Still pressing my head into Jason, I pull his legs out from under him.

10 Straddling Jason's legs with my legs, I chop away at his face with mild punches. The moment he drops his hands to the ground in an attempt to regain his footing, I drop a solid right cross.

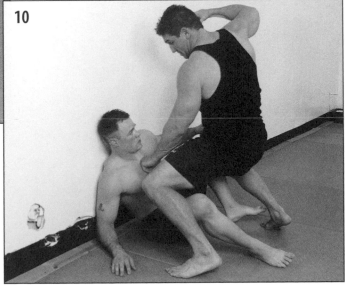

Turning Opponent for Single-Leg Wall Takedown

The single-leg takedown is not any more or less effective than the double-leg takedown when you've got your opponent trapped up against the fence, but it generally puts you in a better position to take your opponent's back once you've got him on the ground.

1 While pummeling with Jason in the clinch, I wrap my left arm tightly around his right arm and grab on to his biceps with my right hand. Jason pushes his weight into me and drives me up against the wall, straightening my body out. It is now difficult for me to turn from side to side or drop low for Jason's legs.

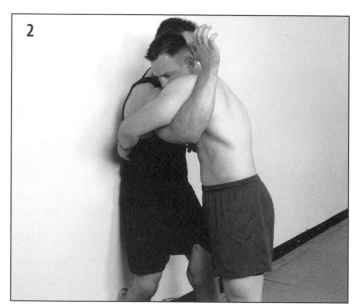

2 Pushing on Jason's left biceps with my right hand, I create enough space to slip my arm underneath his armpit.

3 Turning my hips in a counterclockwise direction, I swim my right arm toward the wall while tugging on Jason's right arm with my left arm.

4 As Jason's back is turned against the wall, I drive my weight into him to straighten out his body and limit his mobility.

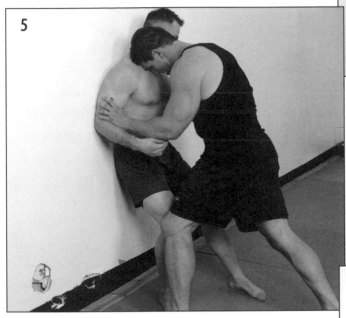

5 Driving my right shoulder into Jason's body, I turn my left hip out just enough to grab his right biceps with my left hand. Pinning his right biceps to the wall, I then grab his left biceps with my right hand.

6 As I keep Jason pinned to the wall by pressing on his arms, I place my right foot behind Jason's left leg and place my left foot in front of Jason's left leg.

7 In a quick motion, I bend at the knees and grab Jason's left ankle with both hands.

8 Driving my right shoulder into Jason's left leg just above his thigh, I pull up on his left ankle with my hands, forcing his body to the ground.

9 Gripping Jason's calf with my right hand, I scoop my left arm underneath his left leg and grab on to his shin with my left hand. I keep pulling on Jason's leg so he can't regain his footing before I can bring my weight down on his body.

10 Pinning Jason's left leg to the ground with my right hand, I let go of his leg with my left hand and shoot my body forward.

11 Stepping over Jason's legs with my left leg, I place my left hand on his shoulder to keep him down as I throw punches with my right hand. It is important to note that if your opponent rolls to his stomach to keep from getting hit, quickly take his back and sink in a rear naked choke, which you will learn about in the section on the rear mount.

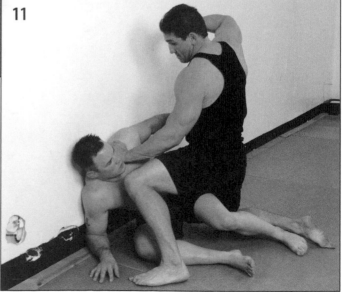

Fifty-Fifty Elbow

It can sometimes be difficult to reach down and snatch one or both of your opponent's legs when you have him trapped up against the fence. If this is the case, it never hurts to soften him up with a couple of hard elbow strikes to get his mind off defending your takedowns.

1 I've got my right arm hooked tightly over Jason left arm. I'm pinning Jason's back against the wall by driving my weight into him and pressing on his right biceps with my left hand.

2 Still pinning Jason's right arm to wall with my left hand, I pull my right shoulder slightly back and lift up my right elbow so it's on the same level as Jason's chin.

3 Snapping my hips in a counterclockwise direction, I whip my right elbow over Jason's left arm and strike his jaw with the point of my elbow.

■ Takedown Defense

The Sprawl

The sprawl is the most effective way to stop an opponent from hauling you to the ground when he shoots in for your legs. Although the move is rather simple, it should be drilled over and over until it becomes second nature.

1 I'm in a fighting stance just inside of striking range.

2 As Jason drops down into his sprinter's stance to shoot for my legs, I also drop my elevation. It is important to note that I have kept my hands up to protect my face.

3 As Jason's body gets closer, I drop my hands to the top of his head to slow his momentum.

4 I slip my left arm over Jason's right shoulder and throw my right arm across his face, cranking his head toward his left shoulder.

5 As I sprawl my legs back and drop my weight down on top of Jason, I keep his face cranked toward his left shoulder by grabbing hold of his left triceps.

6 Driving my weight down, Jason's body is flattened to the ground. It is important to note that this technique should be executed swiftly, all in one movement.

Crucifix Takedown

The crucifix takedown should be performed when your opponent shoots in for your legs and you block his shoot by dropping both of your arms in front of his shoulders. It's a great move because it ends in a submission, but sometimes it can be difficult to pull off. To counter the roll, all your opponent has to do is drop his weight down on top of you. If this should happen, move directly into the guard position.

1 I'm in a fighting stance just inside of striking distance.

2 As Jason drops down into his sprinter's stance to shoot for my legs, I also drop my elevation. It is important to note that I have kept my hands up to protect my face.

3 Going for a double-leg takedown, Jason places his left knee between my legs and his right foot on the outside of my left foot.

4 Before Jason can really drive his body into me, I scoop my arms underneath his armpits. It is important to note that Jason's head is underneath my left armpit.

5—6 Dropping backward, I lift my left leg up between Jason's legs and use it to kick his body over mine as we roll.

7 I come down on top of Jason in the side mount position. My arms are still in front of Jason's shoulders, wrapped underneath his armpits, and Jason's head is still trapped underneath my left armpit. To ensure that his head doesn't slip out from underneath my left armpit, I dig my arms deep under Jason's armpits.

8–9 Posting on my right foot, I shoot my left leg underneath my right leg and scoot my hips toward Jason's head, putting a tremendous amount of pressure on his neck. It is important to note that if your opponent doesn't tap, you can increase pressure on your opponent's neck by locking your hands together.

Hammer-Lock Takedown

When your opponent shoots for a single-leg takedown, the arm he uses to wrap around the inside of your lead leg is going to be exposed. If you can grab a hold of it before he can really sink his arms deep around your leg, the hammer lock should come very naturally.

1 I'm in a fighting stance just inside of striking distance.

2 As Jason drops down into his sprinter's stance to shoot for my legs, I also drop my elevation. It is important to note that I have kept my hands up to protect my face.

3 Jason goes for a single-leg takedown. He plants his right foot on the outside of my left foot and attempts to wrap his left arm around my left leg.

4 Before Jason can wrap his left arm around my left leg, I bend down and grab his left wrist with my right hand.

5 Once I have a tight grip on Jason's left wrist with my right hand, I slip my left arm underneath his left arm and grab my right wrist, creating a figure-four lock on his arm.

6-7 I drop into a backward roll, cranking Jason's left arm toward the ceiling and kicking my left foot up between his legs to force him to roll with me.

8

8—9 Jason lands flat on his back, and my body is on his left side. In order to lock in the submission hold, I need to get to the right side of Jason's body. To achieve this, I continue rolling after Jason comes to a stop, but now I'm going to roll on my left shoulder so that I can kick my legs over Jason's body. As I do this, I keep Jason's arm trapped in a tight figure four.

9

10 Having achieved a side mount position, I pull up on Jason's left arm with my figure-four lock.

10

11 Turning onto my right hip, I post my left foot on the ground by Jason's head and kick my right leg underneath it. This allows me to pull Jason's left shoulder off the ground. To lock in the submission, I pull up on Jason's left arm with my left arm and push on his left wrist with my right hand.

11

14

Top Guard Position

IT'S NICE TO BE ABLE TO HEFT YOUR OPPONENT off his feet, dump him to his back, and then immediately lock in a submission hold. It's nice, but not always possible. These days the majority of MMA competitors are well versed in ground fighting. Instead of floundering on their backs, they quickly wrap their legs around your midsection or waist, capturing you in a position known as the guard. At first it might seem like you have the clear advantage because of your ability to throw downward strikes, but that's not always the case. The man in the bottom guard position can actually be highly offensive if he knows how to utilize his arms, legs, and hips. Instead of lying directly beneath you and allowing you to punch his face, he will constantly shift his hips from side to side. He'll try to escape from underneath you or lock in submission holds such as the arm bar or triangle choke. An opponent who is proficient at fighting from his guard is always moving,

and that not only makes him hard to punch, but also hard to control.

Before trying anything fancy while in your opponent's guard, you first need to get your body and all its parts into the proper positions. Start off by spreading your knees wide. This will give you a solid base and make it difficult for your opponent to roll or sweep you over to your back. Next, drop the weight of your upper body down on top of your opponent. This will hinder your opponent's ability to strike or move his body into positions where he can land submission holds. Lastly, keep your arms on your opponent's chest and stay as balled up as possible. This will make it harder for your opponent to isolate your neck or one of your arms and lock in a hold. Although it will be difficult to get real offensive from here, it is a great position to fall back to whenever your find yourself in trouble.

■ Introduction to Top Guard Position

Coming up on One Foot

Once you have learned how to maintain the basic top guard position, you can start experimenting with other positions while in your opponent's guard. You started off with both knees spread wide on the ground, but if you come up on one foot you can usually create enough space between you and your opponent to land effective punches. Planting one foot on the ground will also give you more options to escape, or "pass," your opponent's guard and transition into a more dominant position such as a side mount. When you come up on one foot, however, it is important to maintain a solid base. If your right foot is planted on the ground, then your balance will be weaker on your left side, and your opponent might try to sweep you in that direction. To prevent this from happening, you must redistribute a larger percentage of your weight over the leg that you have up.

1 I'm in Jason's closed guard. To limit his opportunity to land a submission hold, I keep my head in the center of his chest, my hands on his stomach, and my knees spread wide.

2 Since Jason isn't going for any submissions, I decide to come up to one foot to land some strikes. To achieve this, I dig my hands into Jason's stomach as I lift my upper body off his torso. It is important to note that if you push hard enough, sometimes this will be enough to unhook your opponent's feet behind your back.

3 Still pressing down into Jason's stomach with both hands, I place my right foot on the ground. It is important that you place your foot far enough away from your opposite knee to maintain a solid base, but not so far that it will make it easy for your opponent to turn on his side and hook your foot with his arm.

4 I keep my left hand pressed firmly down into Jason's stomach to limit his ability to reach up and cling on to me or move from side to side.

5 I drop my right fist into Jason's jaw. It is important to note that when you come up like this, your opponent's feet will most likely come unhooked behind your back. Although it is easy to get carried away with striking, you have to be constantly aware of what your opponent's legs are doing. If he starts lifting his knees up to your armpits or tries throwing a leg over your punching arm, it is wise to drop quickly back down into your basic top guard position.

Coming up on Both Feet

Your primary reason for coming up on both feet should be to escape your opponent's guard. It is possible to land some hard punches from this position, but in the process you're going to stretch out your body, which makes you vulnerable to arm bars. You also have to be aware of your legs. If your opponent grabs your feet and pushes with his legs, you're going to end up on your back. Then your opponent can climb on top of you or isolate one of your legs and go for either a heel hook or an Achilles lock. Although it feels natural to stand up, it is important that you understand how your opponent can use your positioning to his advantage before trying such a risky move in a fight.

1 I'm in Jason's closed guard. To limit his ability to land a submission hold, I keep my head in the center of his chest, my hands on his stomach, and my knees spread wide.

2 Since Jason isn't going for any submissions, I decide to come up to both feet to land some strikes. To achieve this, I dig my hands into Jason's stomach as I lift my upper body off his torso.

3 Still pressing down into Jason's stomach with both hands, I place my left foot on the ground.

4 Shifting a portion of my weight to my left leg, I place my right foot on the ground. It is important when standing on both feet in your opponent's guard that you don't lift your body too high. The higher you go, the more you'll have to stretch your body out to land a punch. It will also take longer to drop back into your basic top guard position if your opponent goes for a submission.

5–6 Keeping track of Jason's legs, I raise my right hand and deliver a powerful downward blow.

Closed Guard

Deciding which way to position your body when in your opponent's guard is largely determined by your opponent's positioning. When your opponent keeps his feet locked together behind your back, a position known as the closed guard, his offense will be limited. Because of this, it's a good time to utilize one of the techniques described in this section to pass your opponent's guard. It is also a good time to throw some punches. It is important, however, to always keep track of your opponent's legs. If your opponent starts moving his legs up toward your armpits, it's a good indication that he's hunting for a submission. To avoid getting caught in a submission, it's important to return to your basic top guard position. From there, you can use your elbows to force your opponent's legs back down to your hips.

Open Guard

The open guard is where your opponent unhooks his feet behind your back. It will give you more opportunity to escape your opponent's guard, but you have to be careful because your opponent's ability to move from side to side and create angles just got greater. If your opponent isn't latching on to you with his arms, standing up and backing out is always an option, but the chances are he will have that base covered by holding on to your head or grabbing one of your wrists.

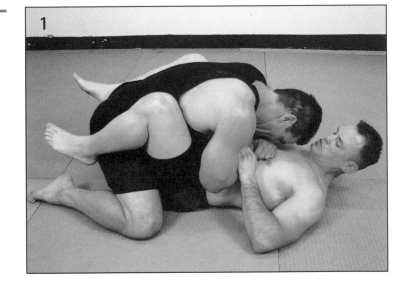

1   I'm in Jason's open guard. To limit his ability to land a submission hold, I keep my head in the center of his chest, my hands on his stomach, and my knees spread wide.

2   With Jason's legs unhooked behind my back, he has more opportunity to use his legs to help land a submission hold. Because of this, I don't want to let my arms stray too far from my body. So instead of going for a punch, I throw a quick right elbow to his jaw and then return to my basic guard position.

Butterfly Guard

If your opponent is playing open guard and manages to get one or both of his feet under your hips, a position known as the butterfly guard, it is a clear indication that he's planning to use his leg or legs to turn your hips over and place you on your back. In order to be successful at this, your opponent will try to bring the weight of your upper body forward so he can more easily lift the lower half of your body. The moment you feel this happening, it is important to shift your weight over your butt and reestablish your base.

1 I'm in Jason's butterfly guard. With both of his legs hooked on the insides of my thighs, I keep my weight back over my butt to hinder him from elevating one of my legs and rolling me over to my back.

2 I place my hands on his knees and force them together.

3 Pressing down on his knees, I hop up to both feet.

4 Still pressing down on Jason's knees with my hands, I slide over them and fall into the mount position and prepare to throw punches with both hands.

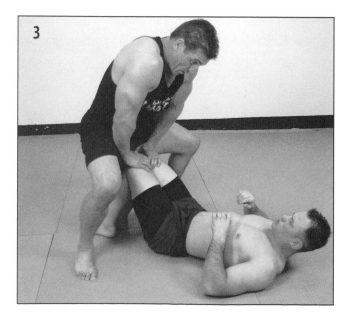

Arm Control

In addition to keeping track of your opponent's legs, it is also important to understand what he's doing with his arms. If your opponent hooks his arms under your arms, there is a good chance he's planning to slip his head underneath one of your armpits and try to take your back. If he over-hooks your arms, he has more ability to move his body into a position where he can go for a submission.

1 I'm in Jason's closed guard. He has both arms hooked over my arms to limit my movement.

2 I'm in Jason's closed guard. He has both of his arms hooked under my arms. To keep him from slipping out from underneath me, I need to keep his head corralled between my arms.

3 I'm in Jason's closed guard. He has chosen to isolate my left arm by over-hooking it with his right arm and clasping his hands together. This gives me an opportunity to punch with my right arm.

■ Passing the Guard

Elbow in Thigh

Although this isn't the most effective way to pass your opponent's guard, it is probably the safest. By pressing down into your opponent's stomach with your hands, you are not only keeping your head out of your opponent's punching range, but you are also locking his hips to the floor. This will make it difficult for him to slide his hips out from underneath you as you make your transition to the side mount position.

1 I'm in Jason's closed guard. To limit his ability to land a submission hold, I keep my head in the center of his chest, my hands on his stomach, and my knees spread wide.

2 Making it hard for Jason to breathe by digging both hands into his stomach, I lift my upper body off his torso.

3 I drive my right elbow into the teardrop muscle of Jason's left thigh just above his knee and begin to force his left leg to the ground.

4 As I come up onto my left foot, my left thigh lifts Jason's right leg and turns his body slightly to his left side. This allows me to place my hand on Jason's left thigh and force his leg all the way to the ground. To keep Jason from sitting up and grabbing on to me, I continue to push into his stomach with my left hand.

5 I place my right shin on Jason's left thigh. From here, I rock from my foot to my knee, driving my right shin across Jason's left thigh.

6 With my right shin still trapping Jason's left leg to the ground, I lean forward and hook my right arm underneath his head.

7 Still using my right shin to trap Jason's left leg to the ground, I step my left leg out from between Jason's legs.

8 Keeping my weight pressed down on Jason and controlling his head with my right arm, I post my left leg behind me.

9 Bringing my right leg underneath my left leg, I assume the side mount position.

Knee in Tailbone

Planting your elbow into your opponent's thigh is a great way to pass the closed guard, but if your opponent has control of your arms it can be difficult to pull off. Planting your knee in your opponent's tailbone is a great alternative. If done correctly, you will have the option of passing into the side mount position or snatching one of your opponent's legs with your arms and dropping back for a heel hook or an Achilles lock.

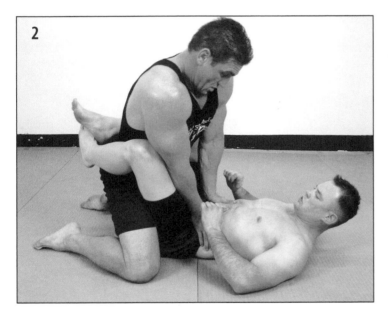

1 I'm in Jason's closed guard. To limit his ability to land a submission hold, I keep my head in the center of his chest, my hands on his stomach, and my knees spread wide.

2 I create space between our hips by posting both of my hands on Jason's stomach and pressing down and away.

3 I come up on my right foot and drive my left knee into Jason's tailbone, further separating our hips. It is important to note that when you do this, your base is going to be weaker on your left side, which leaves you vulnerable for getting swept. To compensate for this, shift more of your weight to your right side.

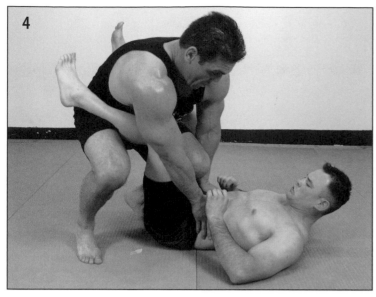

Now that I have created space between our hips, I lift my left knee and place it between Jason's legs.

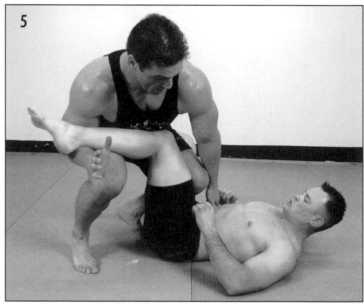

5 I hook my right arm underneath Jason's left leg.

6 Falling down onto my right knee, I whip my body around in a counterclockwise direction and toss Jason's left leg over my head, forcing his body to roll onto his right side. This allows me to quickly move to the left side of his body.

7 I drop the right side of my body down on top of Jason while posting on my left leg.

8 I bring my right leg underneath my left leg and assume the side mount position.

■ Submissions from the Top Guard Position

Heel Hook

If your opponent is familiar with leg sub-missions, this hold isn't the easiest one to lock in. The moment you trap one of your opponent's legs he will most likely push off your butt with his opposite foot in an attempt to free his trapped leg, so you can't afford having sloppy technique. And when you start cranking your opponent's heel over, he will probably roll in the direction that his heel is being cranked to alleviate pressure. If this should happen, focus on rolling with your opponent and securing his leg rather than trying to lock in the hold. Once the two of you have stopped rolling, shift your focus back to locking his heel up tight.

1 I'm in Jason's closed guard. To limit his ability to land a submission hold, I keep my head in the center of his chest, my hands on his stomach, and my knees spread wide.

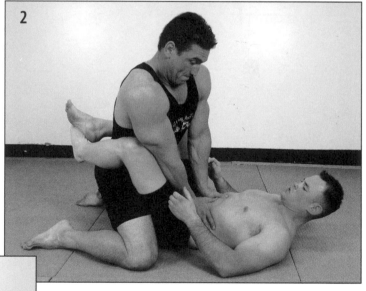

2 I create space between our hips by posting both of my hands on Jason's stomach and pressing down and away.

3 I come up on my right foot and drive my left knee into Jason's tailbone, further separating our hips.

4 Now that I have created space between our hips, I lift my left knee and place it between Jason's legs.

5 Instead of hooking my right arm underneath Jason's left leg as I did when trying to pass his guard, I now grab hold of his left knee with my right hand to keep his leg trapped between my legs as I drop back.

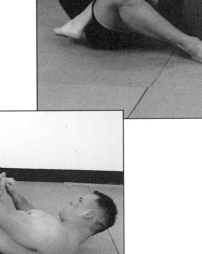

6-7 I throw my right leg over top of Jason's right hip to keep his body pinned to the ground. Then I sit further back, hooking my right arm over Jason's left foot so that his toes are trapped under my armpit. I wrap my right forearm underneath Jason's heel and clasp my hands together. To lock in the submission, I press down on Jason's hips with my heel and pull up on his ankle with my arms.

Heel Hook (Variation)

This technique is best applied when you've dropped back for the heel hook described in the previous move, but your opponent's foot slipped out from underneath your armpit. Instead of letting his leg go, you can move his foot across your body and place it underneath your opposite armpit to go for the same submission. This should be done quickly because the longer you hold on to your opponent's leg the more opportunity he will have to free it.

1 I dropped back for a heel hook from Jason's guard, but his toes slipped out from underneath my armpit.

2 Reaching across my body with my left hand, I grab Jason's heel and pull it over to the left side of my body.

3 Grabbing Jason's ankle with my right hand, I lift my left arm.

4 I wrap my left arm over Jason's foot, trapping his toes in my armpit.

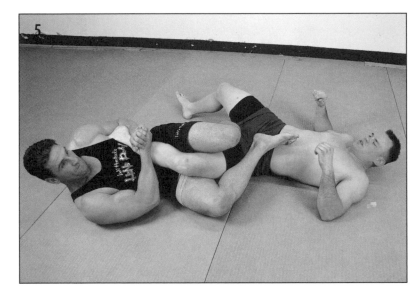

5-6 I scoop my left forearm underneath Jason's heel and then clasp my hands together. To lock in the submission, I push my right foot down into Jason's hips and pull up on his heel with my arms.

Knee Bar

When executing the knee bar from your opponent's guard, it is important to use proper technique and maintain a solid base. If your opponent is able to snatch your leg as you bring it across his body and disrupt your balance, there is a good chance that you will lose the hold as well as the top position.

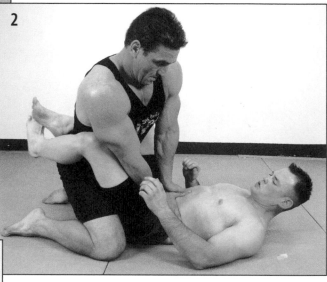

1 I'm in Jason's closed guard. To limit his ability to land a submission hold, I keep my head in the center of his chest, my hands on his stomach, and my knees spread wide.

2 I create space between our hips by posting both of my hands on Jason's stomach and pressing down and away.

3 I come up on my right foot and drive my left knee into Jason's tailbone, further separating our hips.

4 Now that I have created space between our hips, I lift my left knee and place it between Jason's legs. It is important to notice that Jason's left leg is trapped between my right leg and the right side of my body.

5 Keeping my left knee posted on Jason's stomach, I turn my upper body in a clockwise direction so I can hook both arms around Jason's left leg.

6 I push off my right foot and spin my left leg around Jason's left leg, planting my left foot on the left side of Jason's body. I cup my arms tightly around his leg and pull it toward my chest.

7–8 As I drop to my back, I place both feet on the inside of Jason's right thigh and pull his foot to the left side of my head. To lock in the submission, I push off Jason's right leg with my feet, thrust my hips up into his knee, and pull down on his left heel.

Knee Block

The knee block is not as it sounds. You aren't blocking anything—you are still on the attack. Sometimes when you go for a knee bar from the guard position, your opponent will see it coming. To stop the move, he'll bend his knee before you can lock in the hold. If this should happen, abandon the knee bar and immediately go for the knee block. If your opponent tries to straighten his leg to avoid the knee block, transition back into the knee bar.

1 I'm in Jason's closed guard. To limit his ability to land a submission hold, I keep my head in the center of his chest, my hands on his stomach, and my knees spread wide.

2 I create space between our hips by posting both of my hands on his stomach and pressing down and away.

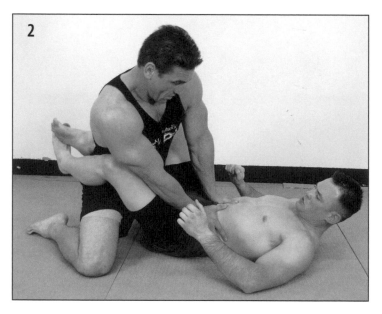

3 I come up on my right foot and drive my left knee into Jason's tailbone, further separating our hips. I then lift my left knee and place it between Jason's legs.

4 I push off my right foot and spin my left leg around Jason's left leg, planting my left foot on the left side of Jason's body. In order to go for the knee bar, I need to cup my arms tightly around his leg, but Jason has bent his leg in defense.

5 I wrap my right arm underneath Jason's left knee.

6 Instead of sitting down on the left side of Jason's body, I sit back directly between his legs. With my right arm still looped under Jason's left knee, I throw my right leg over his left foot. To lock in the submission, I push down on Jason's foot with my right leg and pull up with my arms. Although this submission doesn't look like much, it will put a tremendous amount of pressure on your opponent's knee.

Pro Wrestling

This is a move from the world of professional wrestling that happens to also work in real combat. I know it looks rather silly, but if done right, it can make the toughest fighter quickly tap his hand in submission.

1   I'm in Jason's closed guard. To limit his ability to land a submission hold, I keep my head in the center of his chest, my hands on his stomach, and my knees spread wide.

2   I create space between our hips by posting both of my hands on his stomach and pressing down and away. I come up on my right foot and drive my left knee into Jason's tail-bone, further separating our hips.

3   I lift my left knee and place it between Jason's legs. It is important to notice that Jason's left leg is trapped between my right leg and the right side of my body.

4 Still keeping Jason's left leg trapped between my right thigh and right side, I twist my upper body in a clockwise direction and grab the top of his left foot with my right hand.

5 Pushing down on the top of Jason's left foot with my right hand, I slip my left arm underneath his ankle and grab my right wrist with my left hand, creating a figure-four lock on his leg.

6 Coming down on my right knee and turning my body in a counterclockwise direction forces Jason down onto his belly. To lock in the submission, I pull his ankle up with my left arm while pushing his toes down with my right hand.

Half Boston

This is another move from professional wrestling that works quite well in MMA competition. It's not the highest percentage submission, but when you get the hold locked tight, there are few competitors who can avoid the tap.

1 I'm in Jason's closed guard. To limit his ability to land a submission hold, I keep my head in the center of his chest, my hands on his stomach, and my knees spread wide.

2 I create space between our hips by posting both of my hands on his stomach and pressing down and away.

3 First I come up to my right foot, and then I come up to my left.

4 From the standing position, I place my hands on Jason's knees and then step my left foot over his body, forcing him to belly down on the ground.

5 As I slowly drop Jason's right knee to the ground, I trap his left foot underneath my right armpit by reaching my right arm underneath his leg and clamping down.

6 Sitting my weight down on Jason's back, I arch my back while pulling up with my arms, putting a tremendous amount of pressure on Jason's leg.

Toe Hold

Although you can drop back directly into this submission from your opponent's guard, it can also be used as a backup submission when your opponent pulls his leg out of either the heel hook or the Achilles lock.

1 I'm in Jason's closed guard. To limit his ability to land a submission hold, I keep my head in the center of his chest, my hands on his stomach, and my knees spread wide.

2 I create space between our hips by posting both of my hands on his stomach and pressing down and away.

3 I come up on my right foot and drive my left knee into Jason's tailbone, further separating our hips.

4 I lift my left knee and place it between Jason's legs. It is important to notice that Jason's left leg is trapped between my right leg and the right side of my body.

5 I twist my body in a clockwise direction and grab the top of Jason's left foot with my right hand.

6 I drop back, throwing my right heel on top of Jason's hip to keep him from sitting up into me and blocking or escaping the submission.

7-8 Still holding the top of Jason's left foot with my right hand, I grab his heel with my left hand. To lock in the submission, I push his toes down with my right hand and pull on his heel with my left hand.

15

Side Mount Position

ONCE YOU PASS YOUR OPPONENT'S GUARD AND move into the side mount position, you're ready to get offensive in a big way. The side mount gives you the freedom to strike, land submissions, and transition to other dominant positions such as the mount. Unlike when you were trapped in your opponent's guard, your opponent will have very few opportunities to end the fight. It doesn't mean that he'll be putty in your hands. More likely than not, he'll redirect the majority of his focus and energy into escape, and there are certainly a number of ways he can get an escape. He can roll into you and try to pull you back into his guard, roll away from you, arch his back, or simply buck and trash to create the space that he needs to maneuver his body out from underneath you. In many cases, it's not going to be easy to keep your opponent pinned, so mastering the standard side mount position is a must before trying to go for submissions. There are also several other positions that you can take while in the side mount, and I suggest learning them all because each one has its advantages and its own set of submissions.

■ Introduction to Side Mount

Standard Side Mount

When transitioning into the side mount position from your opponent's guard, expect your opponent to scramble. The best way to come out on top of that scramble is to quickly assume the standard side mount position. Once you have your body and all its parts in place, it generally won't take much energy to keep your opponent down. It's a good position to catch your breath, figure out your next move, and fall back to if you find yourself in trouble.

1 To gain control of Jason's upper body, I wrap my left arm underneath his head and latch on to his left shoulder with my left hand. To keep him from turning into me and trying to pull me back into his guard, I hook my right arm underneath his right leg. To keep him from turning away from me, I press the weight of my upper body down into his torso. My left leg is sprawled back for balance, and my right knee is tucked up near Jason's right hip.

Head and Arm Control

Assuming head and arm control from the side mount position is an excellent way to keep a desperate opponent on his back. Although there are not as many submission possibilities from this position as there are from the standard side mount, there are a few submissions that have been tested time and again at the top levels of MMA competition, including the key lock with legs, arm bar with legs, the side choke, and the chin to chest choke.

1 I'm in standard side mount. With my left arm hooked underneath Jason's head and my left hand latching on to his left shoulder, I have control of his upper body. With my right arm hooked underneath his right leg, I have control of his lower body. I keep the weight of my upper body pressed down into his torso, limiting his movement.

2 I reach my right arm across Jason's body, and then grab his left wrist with my right hand and pin it to the ground.

3 Posting my left leg back, I slide my right leg underneath my left leg and bring it up near Jason's head.

4–5 I slide my right hand up Jason's left arm, behind his head, and then latch on to my right thigh. As I do this, I slip my left hand down Jason's right arm and grab his elbow. This gives me head and arm control from the side mount position.

Knee in Stomach

Placing your knee in your opponent's stomach while in the side mount position has several different benefits. It can be used to make a quick transition to the mount position, set up several different submission holds, and hinder your opponent's breathing and cause him a decent amount of pain. If you obtain this position and your opponent starts to break free, quickly transition to the standard side mount or the mount position.

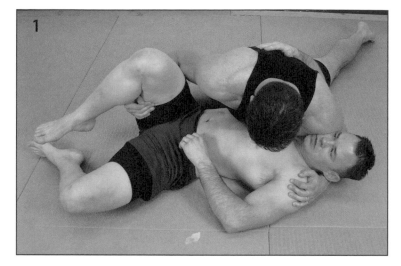

1 I'm in standard side mount. With my left arm hooked underneath Jason's head and my left hand latching on to his left shoulder, I have control of his upper body. With my right arm hooked underneath his right leg, I have control of his lower body. I keep the weight of my upper body pressed down into his torso, limiting his movement.

2 I reach my right arm across Jason's body, and then grab his left wrist with my right hand and pin it to the ground.

3 I place my left hand on the left side of Jason's head, forcing my elbow down into his jaw.

4   Still holding Jason's left wrist to the ground with my right hand, I post on both of my arms and place my right knee into his stomach.

5   With my knee placed in Jason's stomach, keeping his body pinned to the ground, I cup both hands behind his head and pull up.

6   I reposition my knee from Jason's stomach to his sternum to hinder his breath and cause him more pain.

■ Side Mount Submissions

Hammer Lock

The hammer lock is probably the most versatile of all submissions. You can go for it from nearly every position, but slapping it on from the side mount gives you the greatest odds for success. If your opponent tries straightening out his arm to avoid the finish, you can transition directly into the straight arm bar, which is the next submission in this section.

1 I'm in standard side mount. With my left arm hooked underneath Jason's head and my left hand latching on to his left shoulder, I have control of his upper body. With my right arm hooked underneath his right leg, I have control of his lower body. I keep the weight of my upper body pressed down into his torso, limiting his movement.

2 I reach my right arm across Jason's body, and then grab his left wrist with my right hand and pin it to the ground.

3 I place my left arm on the left side of Jason's head, cranking his jaw to his right by applying downward pressure with my elbow.

4 I slip my left arm underneath Jason's left triceps and grab my right wrist. If you have trouble reaching your right wrist with your left hand, do a push-up with your left arm. This will straighten your left arm and make it much easier to grab.

5 I shift my weight to my right side and post my left leg up by Jason's head. This allows me to lift Jason's back off the ground. To put a tremendous amount of pressure on Jason's shoulder, I push his left wrist with my right hand while pulling up on his triceps with my left forearm.

Straight Side Mount Arm Bar

The straight arm bar is another example of how simple can be better. I've seen some of the world's toughest mixed martial arts fighters fall victim to this submission in competition. It can be a little tricky to slap onto an opponent who has phenomenal strength, but once you manage to trap his arm with your arms you've got plenty of options. If your opponent bends his arm down toward his hip to avoid the straight arm bar, then you can apply the hammer lock. If he bends his arm up toward his head, then you can slap on a key lock, which is the next submission in this section.

1 I'm in standard side mount. With my left arm hooked underneath Jason's head and my left hand latching on to his left shoulder, I have control of his upper body. With my right arm hooked underneath his right leg, I have control of his lower body. I keep the weight of my upper body pressed down into his torso, limiting his movement.

2 I reach my right arm across Jason's body, and then grab his left wrist with my right hand and pin it to the ground.

3 I place my left arm on the left side of Jason's head, cranking his jaw to his right by applying downward pressure with my elbow.

4 I slip my left arm underneath Jason's left triceps and grab my right wrist, attempting to apply the hammer lock.

5 As I attempt to apply the hammer lock, Jason straightens his arm out to defend the hold. With my left forearm running just above his elbow and my right hand grabbing his wrist, all I need to do to put unbearable pressure on Jason's elbow and shoulder is push down with my right hand and pull up with my left forearm.

Key Lock

Although the key lock seems rather basic, it is perhaps the most effective submission from the side mount position. I've used it to submit countless opponents in competition, including Sam Adkins, whom I fought in the World Mixed Martial Arts Association's Megafights, held in Atlantic City, New Jersey, on August 10, 2001.

1 Grabbing Jason's left wrist with my right hand, I slip my left hand underneath his left arm and grab my right wrist with the intention of applying a hammer lock.

2 To defend against the hammer lock, Jason straightens out his left arm, so I work to apply a straight arm bar.

3 To defend against the straight arm bar, Jason bends his arm and brings his left hand up by his head.

4 I shift my weight to my right side and post on my left leg to deal with the new development. Still grabbing Jason's left wrist with my right hand, I pull my left arm out from under Jason's arm. I do not let go of Jason's left wrist with my right hand until I have a firm grip on his wrist with my left hand.

5 Now grabbing Jason's left wrist with my left hand, I slip my right hand underneath Jason's left arm and grab my left wrist, creating a figure-four lock on his arm.

6 To lock in the hold, I push Jason's wrist down and back with my left hand while pulling up on his elbow with my right forearm.

Side Choke

If you can isolate one of your opponent's arms while in the side mount position, your submission opportunities are great. You can go for the hammer lock, the straight arm bar, and the key lock. If your opponent is a skilled competitor, he will do everything in his power to keep you from latching on to his arm with your hands. In the process, however, he will most likely put himself in a position to get caught in a side choke.

1 Before I can trap Jason's left arm with a figure-four and apply the key lock, he straightens his arm back out.

2 With Jason having straightened his arm back out, I transition back into the straight arm bar.

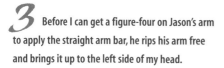 Before I can get a figure-four on Jason's arm to apply the straight arm bar, he rips his arm free and brings it up to the left side of my head.

4 Instead of trying to grab Jason's wrist, I use my right arm to push his left arm up against my shoulder. Then I pinch my head toward my shoulder, trapping Jason's left arm against my neck.

5 I move my left arm over Jason's head and hook it underneath his head. As I do this, I press firmly against the triceps muscle of his left arm with the left side of my neck. It is important to let your opponent's arm fall into the crimp between your neck and jawbone to hold the arm in place. If you try pressing into your opponent's arm using the side of your head, there is a greater chance of him freeing his arm.

6 Still forcing Jason's left arm down with the side of my head, I grab my right biceps with my left hand.

7 To stop Jason from tucking his chin and keeping his arm from falling across his neck, I place my right hand on top of his head and pull it down toward the ground. To sink in the choke, I squeeze my upper body tight.

Loop Choke

When fighting an opponent who has flexible shoulders and elbows, it can take quite some finagling to get him to tap out with a key lock. If this happens to be the case, a good alternative is to force your opponent's arm over his throat and apply a loop choke.

1 I'm attempting to establish a figure-four hold on Jason's left arm to apply a key lock.

2 To defend against the key lock, Jason bends his arm and brings it toward his body.

3 Still grabbing on to Jason's left wrist with my left hand, I help him along by ripping his left arm to his right side.

4 With Jason's left arm directly over his throat, I drop my weight down on top of his arm and hook my left arm underneath his head.

5 Keeping downward pressure on Jason's left arm, I grab my right biceps with my left hand.

6 I place my right hand on top of Jason's head and pull down to lift his chin. To lock in the choke-hold, I squeeze my upper body tight.

Side Mount Arm Bar

Sometimes the best way to create an opening for a submission hold is to put your opponent in pain, and one of the best ways to put your opponent in pain from the side mount position is to place your knee in his stomach and tug on his head with both hands. When you do this, you're making it doubly hard for your opponent to breathe. His first reaction will generally be to extend his arms and push you off him, and that's when you want to go for the arm bar. I went for this technique while fighting Minoru Suzuki in a Pancrase championship bout. I posted my knee in his gut, secured his reaching arm, stepped my foot over his head, and then dropped into the hold. The crowd got all worked up, thinking the fight had come to an end. It was a classy maneuver, but I forgot one small detail. I didn't squeeze my knees together, and Suzuki escaped. Although I ended up winning the fight, losing the hold reminded me just how important it is to keep your head in a fight. No matter how good a position you're in, the tide of bat-tle can change in an instant if you're not focusing on technique.

1 From a standard side mount position, I place my right elbow on top of Jason's left hip to keep his lower body pinned to the ground.

2 I pull my left arm out from around Jason's head and rake my elbow across his jaw, cranking his head to his left side. This gives me control of his upper body.

3 With my right elbow holding down Jason's hips and my left elbow cranking his neck to the left side, I step my left foot over to the left side of Jason's head. As I do this, his right arm gets trapped between my left thigh and armpit.

4 Posting on my left foot, I place my right knee into Jason's stomach.

5 I release Jason's right arm from under my left armpit and secure his forearm to my chest with my hands.

6 Sitting back with Jason's arm, I secure his wrist with both hands, making sure his thumb is pointing up. With my knees pinched together, I thrust my hips up into Jason's elbow while pulling his arm toward my chest. It is important to note that if your opponent's thumb is not facing up, his arm will generally roll in one direction or the other and you might not get the lock.

Short Side Arm Bar

The short side arm bar is a quick, easy submission that will often fall right into your lap while in the side mount position.

1 From a standard side mount position, I place my right elbow on top of Jason's left hip to keep his lower body pinned to the ground.

2 I pull my left arm out from around Jason's head and rake my elbow across his jaw, cranking his head to his left side. This gives me control of his upper body.

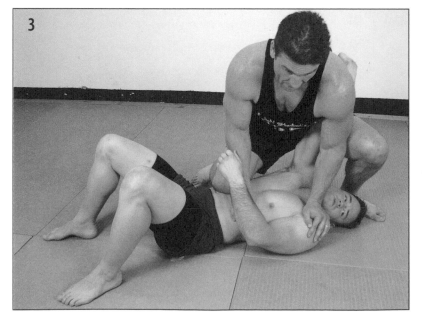

3 I'm posting my right hand on Jason's stomach and my left hand on his left shoulder. Pushing my body upright, I plant my left foot on the ground and my right knee on Jason's stomach. As I do this, Jason's right arm is trapped between my left thigh and armpit.

4 Holding Jason's lower body to the ground with my right knee and hand, I wrap my left forearm underneath his right arm and step my left foot to the left side of his head.

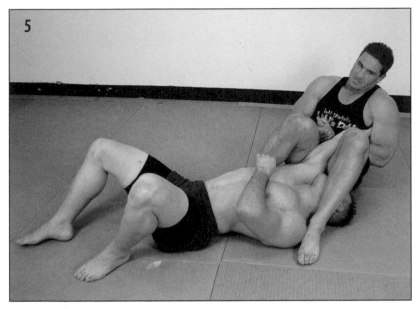

5 Sitting back, I make sure that my left forearm is running underneath Jason's elbow and then clasp my hands together. To lock in the hold, I pinch my knees together, arch my back, and pull up with my arms. It is important to note that although tucking your right shin up against your opponent's side allows you to drop quicker into the submission, throwing your right leg over your opponent will give you better control of his body.

Shoulder-Posted Arm Bar

If your opponent reaches his arms around your head while you're in the side mount position, the shoulder-posted arm bar is right there for the taking.

1 From a standard side mount position, I place my right elbow on top of Jason's left hip to gain control of his lower body.

2 I pull my left arm out from around Jason's head and rake my elbow across his jaw, cranking his head to his left side. This gives me control of his upper body.

3 While cranking Jason's jaw, I place both hands on Jason's left shoulder, trapping his left arm on my shoulder.

4 Posting my right elbow on Jason's torso and my left elbow on his face, I step my left foot over to the left side of his face.

5 Posting on my left leg, I slide my arms up to Jason's triceps muscle just above his elbow and pull his left shoulder off the ground. To lock in the submission, I push my shoulders forward while pulling my arms toward my chest.

Neck Crank

The neck crank is an excellent submission to execute from the side mount position when your opponent is tired or getting sloppy. Although it's an awkward hold to perform, it will put your opponent in a great deal of pain.

1 From a standard side mount position, I place my right elbow on top of Jason's left hip to gain control of his lower body.

2 I pull my left arm out from around Jason's head and rake my elbow across his jaw, cranking his head to his left side. This allows me to slip my right arm inside Jason's left arm.

3 Having brought my right arm inside Jason's left arm, I post on my left leg and turn onto my right side.

4 I cup my left hand around the back of Jason's head and place my right hand on the top of his head.

5 With my left hand cupping the back of Jason's head, I dig my right forearm into Jason's jaw and crank his head to his left side.

6 With my left forearm running behind Jason's head and my right forearm digging into his jaw, I clasp my hands together. To lock in the submission, I pull up with my left forearm and push down with my right forearm. If Jason does not tap, he will end up with a broken neck.

Knee Bar from Side Mount

There are many, many upper-body submissions that you can execute while in the side mount position, but if your opponent is adequately defending his head and arms, it is important to know how to attack his legs. And one of the best leg attacks out there is the knee bar.

1 From a standard side mount position, I place my left arm on the left side of Jason's head and scoop my right arm deep around his right leg.

2 Posting my left hand on Jason's chest, I place my left knee in his stomach and come up on my right foot.

3 Pushing off my right foot, I swing my hips around Jason's right leg and plant my left foot next to my right foot, trapping his leg between my legs.

4 Dropping back to Jason's right side, I place my feet on the inside of his left thigh.

5 I lock my hands together and let my right arm slide up his leg, all the way to his ankle. After clamping my knees together, I thrust my hips into Jason's knee, push off his leg with my feet, and pull his ankle to the right side of my head.

Key Lock with Legs

While grappling and hunting for submissions, it is quite easy to forget about your legs, but they can be quite useful. This is especially true when you have head and arm control in the side mount position. If you have a tight head and arm lock, your opponent will be in a good amount of pain. To alleviate that pain, a lot of times your opponent will put a hand on your chin and try pushing your face away from his body. That's when you want to snatch his wrist, trap his arm under your leg, and apply the key lock. If your opponent tries to resist after you've locked in the hold, he'll end up with a broken elbow and a dislocated shoulder.

1 I have head and arm control in the side mount position. I'm trapping Jason's head underneath my right arm by grabbing on to my right thigh with my right hand, and I'm gripping his right triceps muscle just above his elbow with my left hand.

2 Jason frees his right arm and pushes on my chin in an attempt to create space between us and escape the position.

3 I grab Jason's right wrist with my left hand and force it down.

4 I place my right leg over Jason's right wrist, pinching it between my calf and hamstring.

5 I clasp my hands together behind Jason's head and hook my right foot behind my left leg. To lock in the submission, I pull up on Jason's head with my arms and pull Jason's right wrist down with my right leg.

Straight Arm Bar with Legs

The key lock from head and arm control works great, but if your opponent sees it coming, he will most likely straighten his arm out in defense. If your opponent is strong or putting up a good fight, abandon the key lock and move directly into the straight arm bar. Your opponent's only way of escaping this hold is to turn his arm so that his elbow is no longer posted on your leg, but by doing that he's giving you the opportunity to transition back to the key lock.

1 I have head and arm control in the side mount position. I'm trapping Jason's head underneath my right arm by grabbing on to my right thigh with my right hand, and I'm gripping his right triceps muscle just above his elbow with my left hand.

2 Jason frees his right arm and pushes on my chin in an attempt to create space between us and escape the position.

3 I grab Jason's right wrist with my left hand.

4 I straighten Jason's right arm out over my right thigh.

5 I throw my left leg over Jason's right forearm and trap it under my knee. With Jason's right elbow posted on my right thigh, I force my left leg down and hyperextend his arm.

Straight Arm Bar with Legs (Variation)

If you've tried the straight arm bar several times but your opponent's arm keeps slipping away, try this variation—it's practically foolproof once you get your leg on top of your opponent's arm.

1 I have head and arm control in the side mount position. I'm trapping Jason's head underneath my right arm by grabbing on to my right thigh with my right hand, and I'm gripping his right triceps muscle just above his elbow with my left hand.

2 Jason frees his right arm and pushes on my chin in an attempt to create space between us and escape the position.

3 I grab Jason's right wrist with my left hand.

 I straighten Jason's right arm out over my right thigh.

I lift my right leg and place my ankle on top of Jason's wrist.

 I hook my left knee over my right foot.

Clasping my hands together and pulling up on Jason's head, I force my right ankle down on Jason's wrist. It is important to note that with this hold it doesn't take much to break your opponent's elbow, so be careful when practicing this move with your training partners.

Near Side Choke

When you have head and arm control in the side mount position, a lot of times your opponent simply won't let you bring his arm down and trap it under your leg. If you've tried to go for both the key lock and the straight arm bar and had no luck, the side choke is a great alternative. It's not a finishing submission all of the time, but throughout the years I've choked out more than a few opponents over in Japan with this technique.

1 I have head and arm control in the side mount position. I'm trapping Jason's head underneath my right arm by grabbing on to my right thigh with my right hand, and I'm gripping his right triceps muscle just above his elbow with my left hand

2 Jason frees his right arm and pushes on my chin in an attempt to create space between us and escape the position.

3 Instead of grabbing Jason's right wrist, I push on his right elbow and force his arm down over his face and throat.

4 Before I remove my hand from his elbow, I tuck my head up against the triceps muscle of his right arm to keep it snug over his face.

5 Posting on my left foot, I slip my right leg underneath my left leg and turn my hips toward the ground.

6 With the side of my head still pressed tightly against Jason's triceps, I grab my left biceps with my right hand.

7 I place my left hand on top of Jason's head and pull down to bring up his chin, and then I squeeze my upper body tight, locking in the chokehold.

Chin-to-Chest Choke

When you have head and arm control in the side mount position and have gone for the key lock, the straight arm bar, and the side choke, yet none of them have worked, try the chin-to-chest choke. Although it's more of a smother than a choke, it can be quite effective, especially if you have some strength. Some people might consider it a low-percentage move, but when Mark Coleman applied it to Dan Severn in UFC 12, held on February 12, 1997, it caused Severn so much discomfort that he tapped his hand in submission even though the championship belt was riding on the line.

1 I have head and arm control in the side mount position. I'm trapping Jason's head underneath my right arm by grabbing on to my right thigh with my right hand, and I'm gripping his right triceps muscle just above his elbow with my left hand.

2 Posting my right leg out in front of me, I grab my left forearm with my right hand.

3 To lock in the submission, I lean my weight back into Jason's sternum while pulling up on his head with both arms. This forces Jason's chin to touch his chest, not only causing him a great deal of pain, but also obstructing his ability to breathe.

Shoulder Crank

When you have head and arm control in the side mount position and your opponent has his arms wrapped tightly around your body to avoid the key lock and straight arm bar, employing the shoulder crank is a great way to force him to tap out in a hurry.

1 I have head and arm control in the side mount position. I'm trapping Jason's head underneath my right arm by grabbing on to my right thigh with my right hand, and I'm gripping his right triceps muscle just above his elbow with my left hand.

2 With Jason's right forearm trapped underneath my left armpit, I run my left forearm underneath his right elbow.

3 Keeping my left forearm underneath Jason's right elbow, I clasp my hands together.

4 Arching my back, I drive my left forearm up into Jason's elbow, putting a tremendous amount of pressure on his shoulder.

16

The Mount Position

THE MOUNT POSITION IS LIKE THE SIDE MOUNT position in that you can focus a whole lot on offense and worry very little about defense. The main thing that should be on your mind, other than dropping hard punches to your opponent's face and locking in a submission hold, is not letting your opponent escape from underneath you. When you've got the mount, nine times out of ten escape will be your opponent's primary objective. He'll try bucking his hips to shake you off. He'll try escaping out between your legs. He'll try kicking his legs over your shoulders to rip you to your back. He'll try hooking one of your arms and legs and rolling you to the side. He'll most likely try anything he can think of, especially if you're capitalizing on your ability to throw punches.

For these reasons, it's important not to get too overzealous. Just because you're straddling your opponent doesn't mean the fight is won. In the Lion's Den, I teach my fighters how to weather a storm of punches when mounted. I throw on a pair of boxing gloves, climb on top of them, and then throw bombs at their face and head. If they don't find a way to escape from underneath me, they discover what it's like to eat several dozen shots. A lot of camps have adopted this training strategy, and fighters are getting tougher. It hasn't made the mount any less danger-

ous, but it has certainly made the mount a harder position to keep. So before focusing too heavily on getting the knockout or the tap, it is important to first gain control of your opponent's body when you have him mounted.

■ Introduction to the Mount

The Grapevine

If your opponent is a scrambler, the safest way to gain control of his body while in the mount position is to utilize the grapevine. To achieve the grapevine position, you want to lace your legs underneath your opponent's legs and hook your feet around the inside of your opponent's calves. To reduce your opponent's ability to arch or roll, you want to force his legs apart with your feet. Then, with your lower body hooked to your opponent's lower body, you want to use the anchor to slightly arch your back. This will drive your hips down into your opponent's abdomen and not only make it more difficult for him to escape, but also harder to breathe. Although there aren't a ton of submissions that you can lock in from here, it's a great position from which to torture your opponent by throwing punches to the side of his head and ribs.

I used the grapevine to torture Alexander Otsuka in the Pride Fighting Championships. It wasn't until I tried to slap on a key lock that he was able to shake me off the mount.

1 This is the grapevine position from the mount. My legs are laced underneath Jason's legs, and my feet are hooked just below his knees, spreading his legs apart. My body is positioned directly on top of Jason, my arms spread out wide for balance. This position allows me to slow the pace of the fight and figure out my next move.

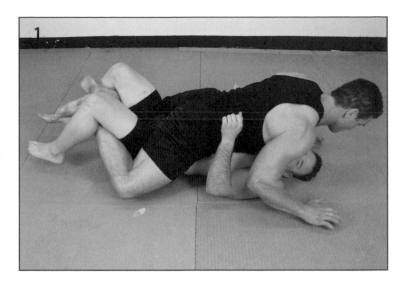

High Mount

If you want to be more offensive while straddling your opponent, the high mount is the way to go. By inching your knees up toward your opponent's armpits, numerous submission opportunities will open up, including the mounted triangle and the arm bar. If you sit up in this position, you will also have the leverage to drop some hard punches to your opponent's face. But there is a trade-off. Now that your opponent's legs are free, his ability to move will increase. This will give him more opportunity to escape. To narrow his options, you want to clamp your knees tightly into his sides, making it hard for him to spin. But sometimes this isn't enough, which is why you have to be really aware of your opponent's movements when in the high mount. If you're fighting a real powerful wrestler and he does manage to spin, you have to loosen you legs before he spins to avoid getting thrown to the side to which he is spinning. By loosening your legs, your opponent will turn underneath you and belly down on the ground. Once this happens, you'll be in a perfect position to sink in a rear naked choke, which you will learn about in the section on taking your opponent's back.

1 This is the high mount. My knees are up near Jason's armpits, and I'm pinching my legs together to hinder Jason's ability to roll underneath me. As you can see, this is the perfect position from which to throw downward punches to the face.

Side Mount to Mount

Although the side mount is a very strong position, full of striking and submission opportunities, you will eventually go up against an opponent who is a master at pulling you back into his guard. It can be frustrating, working so hard to get into the side mount position and then losing it in a blink of an eye. If you run into this dilemma, transitioning from the side mount to the mount position can often solve your problems. The number of submissions you can land from here is going to diminish, but your ability to land effective strikes will increase.

1 From a standard side mount position, I place my right elbow on top of Jason's left hip to gain control of his lower body.

2 Keeping my hips low, I place my right knee on top of Jason's stomach.

3 I slip my right knee across Jason's stomach and then down to the ground on his left side.

4 I hook both my feet underneath Jason's legs and spread my arms for balance.

■ Mount Submissions

Arm Bar

When in the mounted position, your ability to throw downward punches at your opponent's face is great. A lot of times this will cause your opponent to panic and extend his arms upward in an attempt to push you off his body. This will set you up perfectly for the arm bar.

1 I'm in the mounted position, clamping my legs together so my opponent can't squirm beneath me and escape.

2 I reach my right arm across my body and grab Jason's right triceps muscle with my right hand. Then I drop my left hand down to Jason's jaw and crank his head to his left.

3 Still cranking Jason's head to his left, I rotate my hips so that they're turned into Jason's right arm and come up on my right foot.

4 Still posting my left arm on Jason's jaw, I bring my left foot around to the left side of his face. As I do this, I secure Jason's right arm to my chest with my right arm.

5 As I sit back, I force Jason's body to the ground with my legs and trap his arm by pinching my knees together. After letting my hands slide up to his wrist, I thrust my hips into Jason's elbow and pull his hand down toward my chest.

1 I'm in the mount position, arms spread out wide for a solid base.

2 Posting my left elbow on the ground, I draw back my right fist like I'm going to punch Jason in the face. Jason's reaction is to shield his face with his right arm.

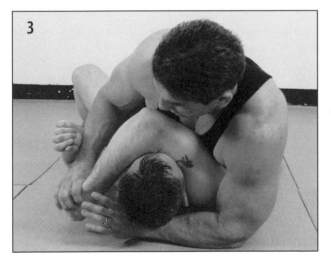

Arm Triangle

Although the arm triangle is relatively easy for your opponent to block, it is one of the safest submissions to attempt while in the mounted position.

3 Instead of punching, I grab Jason's right wrist with my right hand and force it down to the left side of his head. Then I slip my left arm underneath Jason's head and grab his right wrist with my left hand. This locks his right arm over his face and throat.

4 I slip my right forearm underneath Jason's right arm and grab my left biceps. To lock in the choke, I simply squeeze my upper body tight.

1 I'm in the mount position, arms spread out wide for a solid base.

Leg Triangle

You can lock in the leg triangle and remain in the mounted position, but rolling over to your back will allow you to cinch the hold tighter. If you decide to roll and your opponent escapes, you want to immediately assume the bottom guard position, which is described in the last section of this book.

2 Posting my left elbow on the ground, I draw back my right arm like I'm going to punch Jason in the face. Jason's reaction is to shield his face with his right arm.

3 Instead of punching, I grab Jason's right wrist with my right hand and force it down to the left side of his head.

4 I slip my left arm underneath Jason's head and grab his right wrist with my left hand. This locks his right arm over his face and throat.

5 Pulling Jason's right wrist behind his head forces his body onto his left side.

6 Keeping Jason's right wrist trapped behind his head, I come up on my right foot.

7 Posting on my right arm, I slip my right leg between Jason's left shoulder and his right arm.

8 As I roll onto my right shoulder, I hook my left knee over my right foot.

9 I grab Jason's right wrist with both hands and pull it up to my chest. Tightening my legs around Jason's head will lock in a chokehold, but to be on the safe side I thrust my hips up into his right elbow and pull his right wrist to my chest, locking in an arm bar to boot.

Toe Submission

When you're having no luck isolating your opponent's head or arms while in the mounted position, the toe submission is a great backup because many competitors tend to forget about their lower body. This is especially true when they are mounted. But when you go for the toe submission, go for it. If your opponent sees it coming and straightens out his leg, you're not going to land the hold.

1 In the mounted position, I stretch Jason's body out with a grapevine. My legs are laced underneath his legs, and my feet are hooked around the inside of his legs, spreading them apart.

2 Turning onto my left side, I pull Jason's foot toward my head with my right foot.

3 Keeping my weight planted firmly on top of Jason, I reach down and grab the top of his left foot with my right hand. Once I snatch his foot with my hand, I kick my right leg out behind me for balance.

4 Moving my right shin to be pinched between Jason's left hamstring and calf, I pull on his foot as I drop down to my left hip on the right side of Jason's body. This forces Jason's belly down on the ground.

5 Sitting with both buttocks on the ground, I grab the top of Jason's left foot with both hands. To lock in the hold, I pull the top of Jason's foot toward my chest with my hands while pushing my right shin behind Jason's knee.

17

Rear Mount Position

THE REAR MOUNT IS ONE OF THE MOST dominant positions in MMA competition because of the rear naked choke. There are other solid submissions that you can lock in from the rear mount, but nothing nearly as conclusive. Because of this, many competitors have spent a good deal of time and energy learning how to defend against the rear naked choke. So, if you have your opponent's back, expect a battle. The last thing you want while engaged in this battle for the choke is to lose the rear mount. To keep this from happening, it is wise to secure your position before going for the choke. There are several different rear mount positions that you can secure. Some will give you better control over your opponent than others, but it's important to learn all of them because you never know how your opponent will be positioned when you take his back. He could be lying flat on his belly, balled up on the ground, or lying on top of you with his chest facing the sky. No one rear-mount position will work for all of these scenarios, so you should give them all an equal amount of attention during practice.

■ Introduction to Rear Mount

Grapevine

If your opponent is balled up underneath you when you take his back, the best way to gain control of him is to flatten his body out on the ground using a grapevine. After you do this, your legs will be positioned underneath your opponent's thighs, elevating his legs off the ground. This will not only put your opponent in pain, but it will also make it very difficult for him to get back to his knees. To further reduce your opponent's mobility and cause him even more pain in the grapevine, use your anchored legs to arch your back and drive your hips down into your opponent's lower back. This will put you in a great spot to take a breather, fire some punches to the sides of your opponent's head, and figure out your next move. But with your hips riding low on your opponent's back, sinking in the rear naked choke from here will be quite a reach.

1   I have a rear mount on Jason. With my arms posted on his back, I have the majority of my weight directly over his hips to keep his body on the ground. To limit his side-to-side movement, my legs are pinched tightly together on either side of his hips.

2   Posting my hands on Jason's back and keeping the majority of my weight over his hips, I wedge my left foot between Jason's thigh and side and slip it down between his legs.

3   With my left foot between Jason's legs, I keep my hands posted on his back and wedge my right foot between Jason's right thigh and side and slip it down between his legs.

4 With both of my legs laced between Jason's legs, I make sure the majority of my weight is directly over Jason's hips.

5 I reach my arms underneath his arms and grab his wrists.

6 To complete the grapevine, I straighten out my body by arching my back and rolling my hips forward. This flattens Jason's body to the ground.

7 Side angle: With his legs trapped between my legs, it will be very hard for him to come back up to his knees.

Rear Mount, Legs Over

If your opponent is already belly down on the canvas when you take his back, sometimes it can be hard to wedge your legs underneath his legs for the grapevine. When this is the case, placing your legs over your opponent's legs is a good option. In addition to making it difficult for your opponent to rise up to his knees, this position will also allow you to inch your body up your opponent's back so you can begin working for the rear naked choke.

1 With my hips directly above Jason's hips, I keep my knees on the outsides of Jason's legs and hook my feet around his calves just below his knees. To take away his base, I spread his legs using my feet and hook my arms underneath his armpits.

Rear Mount, Side

If you end up off to one side of your opponent's body when taking his back, utilizing the control positions below will make for a relatively easy transition to one of the other rear mount positions. Some competitors like to purposely position themselves off to one side of their opponent's body because it opens them up for a number of submissions and strikes, but it can be dangerous because your opponent will have more options to escape from underneath you.

1 With Jason lying belly down on the canvas, I crank his chin to his left side with my right forearm and grab his left triceps with my right hand. I place my left arm across his lower back and drop the weight of my upper body down on his back to keep his body to the ground. My right knee is tucked up by Jason's right arm, and my left leg is sprawled back for balance.

Rear Mount, Side (Variation)

1 To obtain the side rear mount with Jason balled up on the ground, I position my hips above his hips. Placing my upper body snug against Jason's back, I reach my left arm underneath his left side and reach my right arm over his right shoulder. My right knee is digging into Jason's right hip, and my left leg is posted behind Jason's legs for balance.

Rear Mount, Opponent on Top

If your opponent manages to roll you over while you're in the rear mount, don't abandon the position. As long as your opponent's chest is facing the sky, you still have the rear mount. When in this position, your main concern should be keeping your opponent from spinning in your grasp. If your opponent manages to corkscrew his body, the two of you are going to be belly to belly in your guard, and you will have lost your dominant position. To prevent this from happening, you must learn how to properly latch on to your opponent while lying on your back in the rear mount position.

1 With Jason's back to my chest, I gain control of his lower body by throwing my legs over his hips and placing my feet between his legs. To gain control of Jason's upper body, I wrap my left arm around the left side of his head and hook my right arm underneath his right armpit. I clasp my hands together and tighten down.

■ Rear Mount Submissions

Rear Naked Choke

When you take your opponent's back, sinking in the rear naked choke should be your number one goal. If you learn all its subtleties, it will most likely be the highest percentage submission in your arsenal. I used it to tap out Felix Lee Mitchell in the Ultimate Fighting Championship, and I have used it countless times to submit my opponents in Pancrase. It's an outstanding submission because once you have it sunk, your opponent only has two options—tap in defeat or pass out.

1   I have the rear mount on Jason. With my arms posted on his back, I have the majority of my weight directly over his hips to keep his body on the ground. To limit his side-to-side movement, my legs are pinched tightly together on either side of his hips.

2   I hook both my legs underneath Jason's legs and then slip my arms underneath his armpits and grab his wrists.

3   To flatten Jason out on the ground, I arch my back and roll my hips forward.

4 Still arching my back and driving my hips down into Jason's back, I tug my right arm out from underneath Jason's right armpit.

5 After I dig my right hand across Jason's throat, I pull my left arm out from underneath Jason's left armpit.

6 I grab my left biceps with my right hand.

7 I place my left hand on the back of Jason's head and push down. To lock in the choke, I squeeze my arms tight.

Rolling Arm Bar to Front

The rolling arm bar to the front is a great submission when your opponent is balled up tightly on the ground and you can't get both of your feet under his legs to spread him out in a grapevine. The key to making this move a success is to really drive your shin and knee into the back of your opponent's head.

1 I'm in the rear mount position. I have my legs laced between Jason's legs, my arms are hooked underneath his armpits, and I'm grabbing his wrists with my hands.

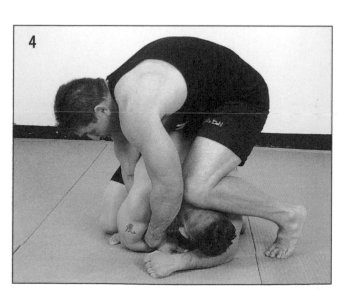

2 Keeping my weight over Jason's hips, I pull my left arm out from underneath his left armpit.

3 I reach over Jason's right shoulder with my left arm and grab my right wrist with my left hand, creating a figure-four lock on Jason's right arm.

4 Turning my hips in a clockwise direction, I pull my left leg out from between Jason's legs and place my knee on the back of his head. As I do this, I post my right foot on the ground underneath Jason's stomach.

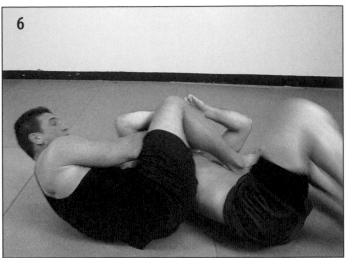

5-6 As I roll to my left side above Jason's head, I'm going to force Jason over onto his back. I accomplish this by driving his head underneath his body with my left knee and pulling up on his lower body with my right leg. As I execute this scissor-like motion with my legs, I keep my arms locked tight on Jason's right arm.

7 As Jason's legs come over his head and he lands on his back, I quickly throw my left leg over his face to keep him from sitting up.

8 Clamping my knees together, I pull Jason's wrist into my chest while thrusting my hips up into his elbow.

Rolling Arm Bar to Side

When your opponent is balled up on the ground, he'll do everything in his power to stop you from slipping your legs between his legs and stretching him out in the grapevine. Sometimes he'll press his thighs tightly up against his chest, and other times he'll hook an arm around one of your legs to prevent you from wedging between his legs. If he does the latter, he just set you up to execute the rolling arm bar to side.

1 I'm in the rear mount position. I have my legs laced between Jason's legs, my arms are hooked underneath his armpits, and I'm grabbing his wrists with my hands.

2 I pull my right leg out from between Jason's legs and post my right foot next to Jason's right shoulder. Instinctively, Jason wraps his right arm around my right leg and pulls it forward.

3 To trap Jason's right arm around my right leg, I post my right hand above his head and drop my right knee down to the back of Jason's head.

4 Reaching my left arm underneath Jason's left biceps, I grab my left forearm with my right hand, creating a figure-four lock on Jason's left arm.

5 I hook my left foot underneath Jason's left leg, and then roll on to my right side.

6 By tugging on Jason's arm with my left arm and pulling on his left leg with my left foot as I roll, I force Jason onto his back.

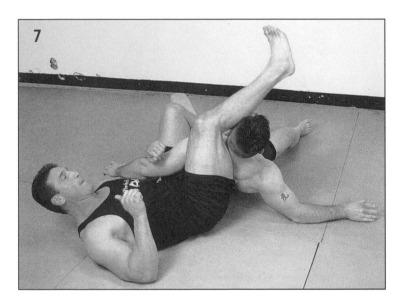

7 Keeping Jason's left arm snug to my chest with my left arm, I quickly throw my right leg over his face and force his head to the ground.

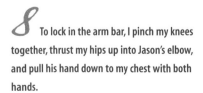

8 To lock in the arm bar, I pinch my knees together, thrust my hips up into Jason's elbow, and pull his hand down to my chest with both hands.

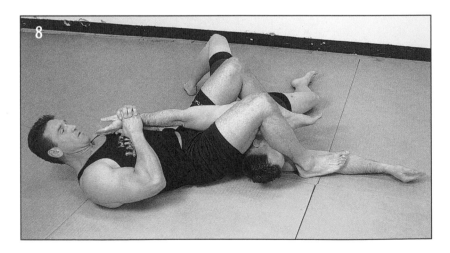

Rolling Side Arm Bar

To sink in a rear naked choke, a lot of times you will have to release the grapevine and work your body up your opponent's back. If your opponent comes up on his knees every time you do this, executing the rolling side arm bar is a good way to catch him by surprise.

1 I'm in the rear mount position. With my arms posted on Jason's back, I have the majority of my weight directly over his hips to keep his body on the ground. To limit his side-to-side movement, my legs are pinched tightly together on either side of his hips.

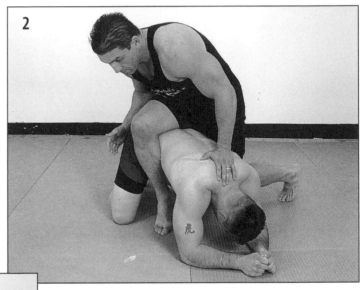

2 Turning my hips in a clockwise direction, I plant the toes of my left foot on the floor and dig my left knee into the left side of Jason's body. My right leg is wrapped around Jason's right side.

3 Keeping my weight centered on Jason's back, I wrap my left arm over Jason's left shoulder and my right arm over his right leg. It is important to note that my right leg is still pressed up against Jason's right side.

4–5 I hook my right leg underneath Jason's body, reach my right arm between his legs, and grab around his head with my left arm. Pushing off slightly with my left foot, I tuck my head underneath Jason's body and roll over onto my back.

6 Pushing Jason's body to the ground with my right leg, I quickly throw my left leg over his head to stop him from sitting up.

7 I straighten out Jason's arm and slide my hands up to his wrist. To lock in the arm bar, I pinch my knees together, thrust my hips into his elbow, and pull his hand into my chest.

Banana Split

When an opponent is balled up tightly on the ground, you can usually slip one of your legs between his legs with relative ease. Getting your other leg in, however, can be a little trickier. Realizing your intentions, your opponent will put up a fight. If you've tried everything but your opponent just won't let that second leg through, the banana split is a great submission to employ.

1 I have the rear mount on Jason. With my arms posted on his back, I have the majority of my weight directly over his hips to keep his body on the ground. To limit his side-to-side movement, my legs are pinched tightly together on either side of his hips.

2 Turning onto my left side, I hook my left leg between Jason's legs and hook my left foot over Jason's left foot.

3-4 I reach my left arm underneath Jason's right leg and my right arm over his right leg, clasping my hands together behind his right hamstring. Rolling over to my back, I pull Jason's right leg. As I do this, I keep my left foot hooked over Jason's left leg.

5 With my left leg still hooked over Jason's left leg, I throw my right leg over my left foot. This traps Jason's left leg between my legs. To lock in the submission, I push with my legs and pull with my arms, spreading Jason's legs and separating his hips.

Toe Hold

The toe hold submission requires the same positioning as the banana split. Your opponent is balled up underneath you, and you have one leg laced between his legs. It's a good hold to go for if your opponent is giving you time to work, but it's going to be hard to land if your opponent desperately tries to turn his body toward you.

1 I have the rear mount on Jason. With my arms posted on his back, I have the majority of my weight directly over his hips to keep his body on the ground. To limit his side-to-side movement, my legs are pinched tightly together on either side of his hips.

2 Keeping my hands posted on Jason's back, I slip my left foot between Jason's legs.

3 Coming down on my left side, I slip my left leg deep between Jason's legs and place my left foot over the top of his left calf.

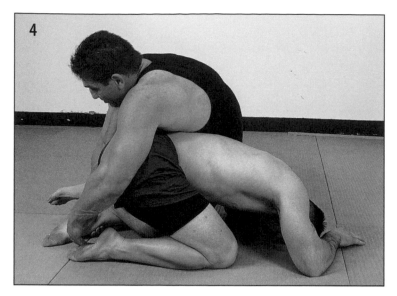

4 Sitting down on the left side of Jason's body, I keep his hips trapped underneath my left armpit as I reach down and grab the top of his left foot with both hands. It is important to note that my left leg is still on top of Jason's left leg.

 Leaning back, I pull up on the top of Jason's left foot, pinching my left leg between Jason's left calf and hamstring.

6 I throw my right leg on top of my left foot. To lock in the submission, I push my left leg into Jason's leg while pulling on the top of his foot with both hands. This will separate his knee if he does not tap.

Neck Crank

The neck crank works great when your opponent is blocking the rear naked choke by keeping his chin tucked against his chest. When you employ this technique, your opponent will usually lift his chin because of the pain, in which case you can sink in the rear naked choke. If your opponent keeps his chin tucked, slowly increase pressure until he taps. It is important to note that this submission is a neck breaker, and if applied with full force, there's a good chance that you'll cause your opponent serious injury.

1 With Jason's back to my chest, I gain control of his lower body by throwing my legs over his hips and placing my feet between his legs. To gain control of Jason's upper body, I wrap my left arm around the left side of his head and hook my right arm underneath his right armpit. I clasp my hands together and tighten down.

2 I crank Jason's neck to his right side using my left forearm. To stop Jason from reaching up and pulling my left arm down, I grab his right wrist with my right hand.

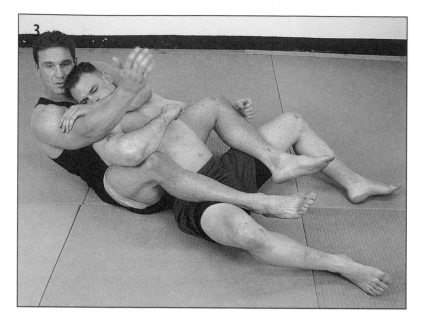

3 Quickly pulling my right arm out from underneath Jason's right arm, I grab my right biceps with my left hand, creating a figure-four lock on Jason's head.

4 With my left forearm still cranking Jason's head to his right, I place my right hand behind his head and lean back. To put an unbearable amount of pressure on Jason's neck, I squeeze my arms tight.

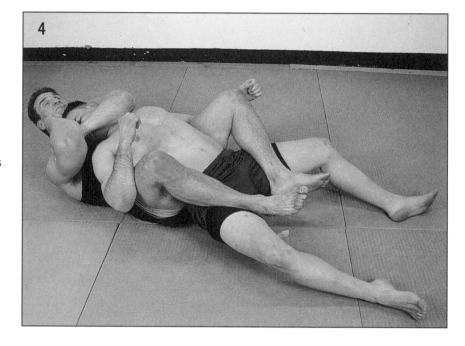

18

Bottom Guard Position

THERE HAD ALWAYS BEEN A GENERAL consensus that when a fight went to the ground, the man on bottom was going to lose. Well, the first Ultimate Fighting Championship shattered that notion in a heartbeat. Millions of people around the world watched Royce Gracie dominate some of the most competent strikers around while lying flat on his back. He did this by corralling his opponents between his legs and then working his body into a position where he could land a submission hold. After that first event, it didn't take long for people to do a complete 180-degree turn. Everyone started learning how to fight from the guard, thinking it was the ticket to victory.

In reality, it wasn't as strong a position as everyone first thought. Don't get me wrong; if you go to your back, the guard is the position you want to assume. It's just that there are more dominant positions out there—basically, any position where you are on top. I proved that when I fought Gracie for the second time in UFC 5. He pulled me into his guard as soon as the fight went to the ground, yet I managed to work him over for thirty minutes straight.

In order to make the guard a dominant position, or even a neutral position, you must keep moving.

Shifting your hips from side to side is your ticket to passing to a more dominant position or landing a submission hold. You might take one or two punches while you move, but it is far better than just lying on your back and trying to cover up. If you just lie there, you'll most likely get knocked out. And if you don't get knocked out, you're going to lose on the judge's scorecards. So if your opponent starts dropping bombs, look at it as a positive thing. In order to land a punch that will do real damage, he's going to need leverage. And to get leverage, he'll need to create space between your bodies. That space is your ticket to movement. It's your chance to take control of the fight.

■ Introduction to Bottom Guard Position

Closed Guard

Locking your feet together behind your opponent's back won't allow you to be highly offensive, but it can allow you to gain control of your opponent's body, get a feel for how he is going to move and react on the ground, or take a breather to decide your next move. Your ability to move from side to side won't be the best, so you don't want to sit in a closed guard without doing anything for long periods of time. If you try this approach, your opponent will slowly wear you down with short, chopping punches. You can, however, turn the closed guard into a more offensive position by inching your legs up your opponent's back toward his armpits. This will allow you to make a much quicker transition to several submission holds such as the arm bar or triangle choke, both of which are covered in this chapter.

Open Guard

The open guard is obtained when you unhook your feet behind your opponent's back. This position will allow you to move your body more freely, but it will also make it easier for your opponent to pass your guard and transition to a more dominant position such as the side mount. To cut down on your opponent's options, keep your feet off the ground and your legs pressed tightly against your opponent's hips. It is also important when maintaining an open guard to move as much as possible. Movement will not only open you up for submission holds, but it will also make your opponent hesitant to sit up and throw punches for fear of extending his arms and getting caught in a submission.

Butterfly Guard

To assume the butterfly guard from the open guard, you want to slip one or both of your feet between your opponent's legs while keeping your knees on the outside of your opponent's body. When transitioning into this position, you should have only one goal—elevating your opponent's lower body so you can turn him over to his back and take the top position. Your opponent will probably distribute the majority of his weight over his legs as soon as you assume this position, so it helps to tie up your opponent's upper body with your arms and keep his weight as far forward as possible. It is also important while working for the reversal to keep your

knees pressed tightly against your opponent's sides. If you let your legs go slack, your opponent will have a relatively easy time passing your guard and transitioning to the side mount position.

1 With both of my feet on the inside of Jason's hips, I can now lift up on either side of his lower body.

Half Guard

If you are lying on your back and manage to trap one of your opponent's legs between your legs, then you're in the half guard position. It's not as strong a position as the full guard, but it's definitely stronger than being in the bottom side mount position. It is possible to reverse your opponent and land submissions from here, as you will see in an upcoming section, but the majority of the time it's safer to trap your opponent between both of your legs and then work for a reversal or a submission.

1 This is the half guard position. I have my legs hooked over Jason's right leg, and I'm controlling his head and arms with my arms.

■ Escaping the Bottom Guard Position

Hip and Out

If you've got an opponent trapped in your guard but he's landing some good punches or defending all your submission attempts, it might be time to start thinking about escaping the bottom position. Although the hip and out technique might seem too simple to work in a real fight, it works surprisingly well, especially when your opponent sits up in your guard to throw punches.

1 I have Jason in my closed guard. My feet are hooked together behind his back, and my hands are posted on his shoulders to control his upper body.

2 Pressing on Jason's right shoulder with my left hand, I come up onto my right hip and slide my left knee across his chest.

3 With my left knee keeping Jason from moving into me, I post my right elbow on the ground. I also move my left hand from Jason's shoulder to the right side of his head.

4 Posting on my right elbow, I place my right foot on Jason's left hip and then kick my left leg out behind me.

5 Still pressing into the right side of Jason's head to keep him at bay, I post on my left foot and kick my right leg back. From here, I can safely stand up. It is important to note that the moment you let go of your opponent's head, he might shoot in for a single-leg takedown, especially if he wants the fight to stay on the ground. In order to avoid the takedown, you must be ready to sprawl.

Sweep 1

There are dozens of ways to sweep your opponent over to his back, but this is definitely one of the better ones. I'd like to say that it's a high-percentage move, but it all depends on your technique. If you do it fast and explosive, it will definitely increase your odds.

1 I have Jason in my closed guard. My feet are locked together behind his back, and I'm holding his head in the center of my chest with both hands.

2 Opening my guard, I turn onto my right hip while posting my right elbow on the ground. As I do this, I reach over Jason's left arm with my left arm.

3 I post my left foot on the ground and hook Jason's left leg with my right leg.

4 To sweep Jason over to his back, I chop into his left leg with my right leg, push off the ground with my left foot so I can drive my left hip up into his body, and tug his left arm underneath my body with my left arm.

5 Having followed Jason over, I land in the mount position with my right leg on the left side of Jason's body and my left leg on the right side of his body.

Sweep 2

This is a good sweep to utilize when your opponent has his arms on your chest and you've secured both of his wrists with your hands. When first learning this move, it can be difficult to remember what to do with your legs once you've got them in place, so it helps to pretend that you are trying to run. The leg that you have posted on your opponent's hip is going to run forward while the leg you have posted on your opponent's leg is going to run backward. If you pull on your opponent's wrists and pretend that you're running for your life, there's a good chance that you'll end up in the mount position.

1 I have Jason in my closed guard. My feet are locked together behind his back, and I'm grabbing his wrists with my hands to control his arms.

2 I jerk Jason's arms to the right side of my head. I then turn onto my right hip, placing my right leg against Jason's left leg and wedging my left knee across his chest.

3 Still controlling Jason's arms to keep him from establishing a base, I chop my right leg into Jason's left leg and drive my left leg into his body, basically making a scissor motion with my legs. This forces Jason over on his back.

4 I follow Jason over, making sure to plant my left leg on the right side of his body and my right leg on the left side of his body.

5 Dropping the weight of my upper body into Jason's stomach and chest, I lace my legs underneath his legs and hook my feet around the inside of his legs just below his knees. I have now assumed the grapevine mount position.

Sliding Out

This is a great technique for escaping from underneath your opponent and taking his back, but when making the transition, it is important that you keep your opponent corralled between your legs. If you allow your opponent to clear both of your legs, he will move directly into the side mount position and assume head and arm control.

1 I have Jason in my open guard. My right hand is cupping the back of his neck, and my left hand is pressed against his right triceps.

2 Turning onto my right side, I push on Jason's right arm with my left hand and slide my head out from underneath his right armpit.

3 Hooking my left hand on the left side of Jason's body, I slide my right foot between Jason's legs.

4 Still hugging Jason's body with my left arm, I plant my left foot on the ground behind me.

5 Posting off my left foot, I work my hips up on top of Jason's back. Once my hips are over Jason's hips, I slip my left leg between Jason's legs.

6 After flattening Jason to the ground with the grapevine, I pull my right hand out from under Jason's right armpit and throw punches to the side of his head.

Elevator

This technique comes into play when you have one or both of your legs laced underneath your opponent's hips. My brother Frank used this technique successfully when fighting Tito Ortiz in the Ultimate Fighting Championship, and I've used it in several of my bouts over in Japan. But before going for the move, you will want to pull your opponent's upper body as far forward as possible so he has less weight riding over his legs. This will make it much easier to lift the lower half of his body for the reversal.

1 I have Jason in my butterfly guard. My right foot is hooked around the inside of Jason's left hip. My left foot is hooked around the inside of Jason's right hip. Both my knees are outside of his body, and I'm grabbing his triceps muscles just above his elbows with both hands.

2 Controlling Jason's right arm with my left hand, I kick my right foot up and to my left, turning Jason over, and his body is forced to my left.

3 I follow Jason over, landing with my knees on the outside of Jason's body.

4 I assume the mounted position by hooking my feet underneath Jason's legs and spreading my arms wide to create a solid base.

■ Bottom Guard Submissions

Hammer Lock

Although the hammer lock is easier to slap on while in the side mount position, it's still a great way to end a fight while lying on your back.

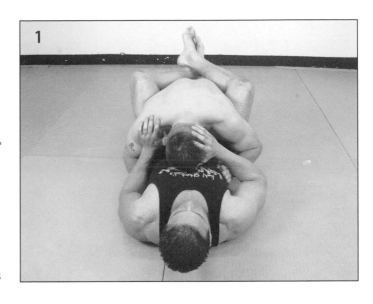

1 I have Jason in my closed guard. My feet are locked together behind his back, and I'm controlling his head and shoulder with my hands.

2 I push on the left side of Jason's head with my left hand, forcing his upper body to my left side.

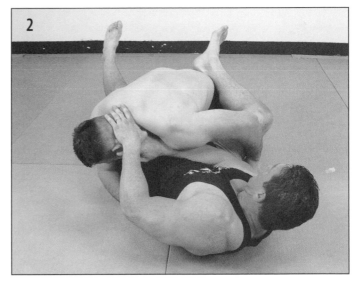

3 Still pushing on the left side of Jason's head with my left hand, I slide my right hand down Jason's arm and grab his left wrist.

4 I slip my left arm underneath Jason's left arm and grab my right wrist. I then hook my feet together behind Jason's back. To lock in the hold, I pull Jason's shoulder down with my left arm and push up on his left wrist with my right hand.

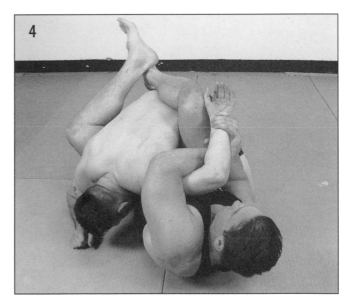

Shoulder-Posted Arm Bar

Although this technique is rather simple, it can be quite effective when your opponent places one of his arms over your shoulder. Your opponent's best defense will be to pull his arm free before you can lock in the hold, so it should be done as quickly and tightly as possible.

1 I have Jason in my closed guard. My feet are locked together behind his back, and I'm controlling his arms by grabbing both of his wrists.

2 I tug Jason's right arm up to the left side of my face with my left hand. To lock his arm in place, I slide my left hand down his arm and grab on to his triceps. I then place my right hand on the right side of Jason's face and push his head to the outside of my body.

3 Running my left forearm across Jason's left triceps just above his elbow, I clasp my hands together. To lock in the arm bar, I pull my arms into my chest.

Over-Hook Key Lock

This technique comes into play when your opponent posts one of his hands on the ground next to your body. When you see the submission, nail it as fast as you can because your opponent will instantly counter the submission by pushing his elbow to the ground or tucking his elbow into his stomach. If he manages to do either of these things successfully, you're not going to get the tap. It is then important to abandon the hold because your face will become a prime target for punches.

1 I have Jason in my closed guard. My feet are locked behind his back, and my hands are controlling his shoulders.

2 I hook my right arm tightly over Jason's left triceps just above his elbow. Then I place my left hand on the left side of Jason's face and force his head to the left side of my body.

3 I clasp my hands together and pull my arms toward the left side of my body. This pulls Jason's left elbow toward the left side of my body while his forearm remains trapped against the right side of my body. This puts a lot of pressure on Jason's elbow and shoulder, causing him to tap.

Triangle

To make this move a success, you must get one of your legs around your opponent's arm and onto his shoulder. You can do this when your opponent tries to punch or when he reaches back for one of your legs. If your opponent isn't making either movement, you can grab his arm and force it down toward your hips. The most difficult part of the move is getting the leg over. In today's mixed martial arts competition, you often see ground fighters attempt this move a dozen or more times throughout the course of the fight, and then, out of nowhere, get their leg over their opponent's arm and lock in the triangle choke. It ends more fights from the guard position than any other submission hold, and it is definitely worth the wait.

1 I have Jason in my closed guard. My feet are locked together behind his back, and I'm controlling his wrists with my hands.

2 Still controlling Jason's wrists with my hands, I turn slightly onto my right side and place my right foot against Jason's left hip to create some space between us.

3 I force Jason's left arm between my legs with my right hand.

4 Still controlling Jason's right arm with my left hand, I throw my right leg over his left arm and wrap it around his head.

5 I bring up my left leg and wrap it over my right foot.

6 Keeping Jason's right arm trapped against my chest with my left hand, I squeeze my left leg down over my right foot and lock in the chokehold.

Arm Bar

This is a great move to go for when your opponent is giving you a little space to work, lifting his body to punch, or trying to sit back and isolate one of your legs. The most important part of this move is speed. The moment your opponent feels your movement, there is a good chance he will either press all his weight down on top of you and smother the hold or lift his knee and drop it down into your face. If you get caught in either such predicament, spin back into the guard position and search for another submission.

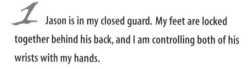 Jason is in my closed guard. My feet are locked together behind his back, and I am controlling both of his wrists with my hands.

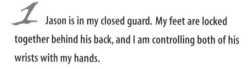 I unlock my feet behind Jason's back and let go of his left wrist. Then I spin on my hips in a counterclockwise direction, reaching for Jason's left leg with my right arm.

3 Hooking my right arm underneath Jason's left leg, I pull my shoulders toward his hips and throw my left leg over to the left side of his head. It is important to notice that I'm still hanging on to Jason's right wrist with my left hand.

4 While securing Jason's right wrist to my chest with my left hand, I push with my legs and force Jason over on his back.

5 Clamping my knees together, I thrust my hips up into Jason's elbow and pull his wrist toward my chest with both hands.

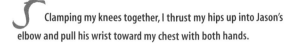

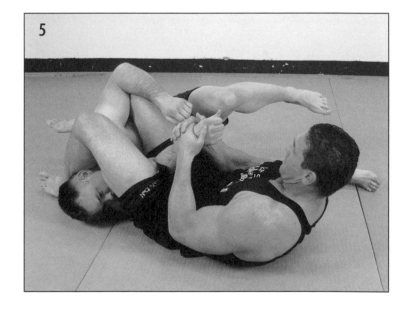

Omoplata

To set up the Omoplata, you need to get one of your opponent's arms down by his hips. Sometimes your opponent will reach back for one of your legs and fall right into the submission. Other times you'll have to grab your opponent's wrist and force it down. Either way, the hold works great once you get it locked in.

1 Jason is in my closed guard. I'm controlling his head with my left hand and his shoulders with my right hand. It is important to notice that Jason has posted both arms on the ground instead of on my chest.

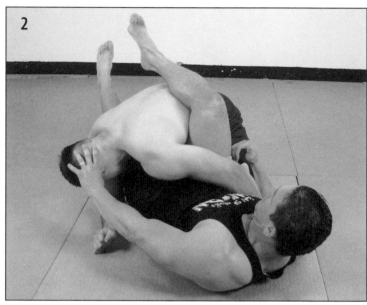

2 Placing my left hand on the left side of Jason's face, I push his head toward the left side of my body.

3 Still pushing Jason's head to the left side of my body with my left hand, I slide my right arm down Jason's left arm and grab his wrist with my right hand.

4 While pressing against Jason's head with my left hand, I bring my left leg out from underneath his body.

5 I plant my left foot on the ground and wrap my right leg over Jason's left shoulder. To keep him from pulling his arm free as I do this, I hold his left wrist firmly against my right thigh with my right hand.

6 I throw my left leg over my right foot.

7 Pushing down with my legs forces Jason's head to hit the ground.

8 Posting on my left hand, I sit up and throw my right arm over Jason's back to keep him from kicking his legs over his head and escaping the hold.

9 I reach forward with my left hand and grab my right shin. With Jason's left arm laced underneath my right leg and trapped between my thigh and hip, I force my right leg down and my hips up. This brings Jason's arm up behind his back and will break his shoulder if he does not tap.

■ Half Guard Submissions

Half Guard Reverse

There are a lot of competitors who are content in the top half guard position because it allows them to throw some decent strikes. If you go up against one of these competitors and have no luck pulling him into your full guard, another option is rolling him over to his back. When executing this technique, it is important that you have a solid hook on your opponent's inside foot before arching into the roll. If you don't, there's a good chance that you'll end up mounted.

1 Jason is in my half guard. I have my right leg wrapped over his right leg to keep him from achieving the side mount position. My right arm is hooked over Jason's left arm and my left arm is looped around his head. To limit his mobility, I have grabbed my right wrist with my left arm above Jason's left shoulder.

2 I tuck my right hand behind my head, pressing my elbow into Jason's shoulder to keep his arm trapped behind my head.

3 Posting my left foot on the ground, I arch my back and thrust my hips up and to my right.

4 Because Jason's left arm is still trapped behind my head, he can't post his arm on the ground and stop the roll.

5 I follow Jason over, landing in his half guard.

Knee Bar Bottom

The knee bar works best from the bottom half guard position when your opponent gives you some space to work, sits up to search for an escape, or tries to get some distance to punch.

1 Jason is in my half guard. I have my right leg over Jason's right leg to keep him from moving into the side mount position. I'm hooking his head with my left arm and controlling his left arm with my right hand.

2 I place my left hand on the left side of Jason's face and push his head to the left side of my body. As I do this, I turn onto my right hip.

3 Still pushing on the left side of Jason's face with my left hand, I hook my right arm underneath Jason's left leg.

4 Pulling my body toward Jason's hips with my right arm, I throw my left leg over his body.

5 I wrap my left arm over Jason's left leg and pull it to the left side of my body.

6 Placing my right foot on Jason's buttocks, I straighten my body out, letting my arms slide up Jason's left leg. To lock the submission, I pinch my knees together, thrust my hips into Jason's knee, and arch back.

Knee Bar Top

When executing the knee bar from the top half guard position, your opponent will probably try to grab your leg as your bring it over his body. The best way to avoid this is to execute the move with good speed and technique.

1 I'm in Jason's half guard.

2 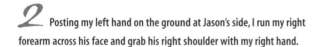 Posting my left hand on the ground at Jason's side, I run my right forearm across his face and grab his right shoulder with my right hand.

3 Posting off Jason's shoulder, I come up onto my left foot, lifting Jason's right leg in the process.

4 Posting my right hand on Jason's stomach, I hook my left arm around Jason's right leg.

5 Pushing off my left foot, I throw my right leg over Jason's body, planting my right foot on the outside of Jason's right leg.

6 Holding onto Jason's right leg with both arms, I drop back.

7 I place my feet on the inside of Jason's left thigh. To lock in the knee bar, I pinch my knees together, thrust my hips into Jason's knee, and pull his foot down to the right side of my head with my arms.

■ Acknowledgments

A SPECIAL THANKS to Jason Pietz and Eric Hendrikx for their help in putting this book together.

◼ About the Authors

KEN SHAMROCK dominated no-holds-barred martial arts competition in both America and Asia. He was the first Superfight Champion of the Ultimate Fighting Championship, the first King of Pancrase, the pioneering Japanese fighting circuit, and is a former WWE superstar. Shamrock has been a guest on many of the major talk shows, including *Late Night with Conan O'Brien* and *Larry King Live*, and he has been featured in *Time*, *Sports Illustrated*, *Black Belt*, and *Muscle and Fitness*.

ERICH KRAUSS is the author of eight books including *Brawl: A Behind-the-Scenes Look at Mixed Martial Arts Competition* (ECW Press, 2002) and *Little Evil: One Ultimate Fighter's Rise to the Top* (ECW Press, 2003). Krauss moved to Pataya, Thailand, in 1997 to train in Muay Thai kickboxing. He now trains at Ken Shamrock's world renowned Lion's Den in San Diego.

◼ About the Photographer

ERIC HENDRIKX started his photography career in the music industry, having been published for his exciting photographs of many of rock and roll's most electrifying musicians, including Zakk Wylde (Ozzy Osbourne, Black Label Society), John 5 (Marilyn Manson, Loser), and Slash (Guns and Roses, Velvet Revolver). His personal interest in Mixed Martial Arts led to several technique-illustrated collaborations with lifelong friend, Erich Krauss, including *Eddie Bravo: Jiu-Jitsu Unleashed*. Hendrikx resides in San Diego, California, and trains with Fabio Santos, one of the world's most respected instructors of Brazilian Jiu-Jitsu.